DATE DUE

MAY 25 '70	

BRODART, CO.   Cat. No. 23-221-003

Trade Policy and Market Structure

Trade Policy and Market Structure

Elhanan Helpman and
Paul R. Krugman

The MIT Press
Cambridge, Massachusetts
London, England

This book was set in Palatino by Achorn Graphic Services and printed by The Murray Printing Co. and bound by Halliday Lithographers in the United States of America.

Library of Congress Cataloging-in-Publication Data

Helpman, Elhanan.
  Trade policy and market structure.

  Includes bibliographies and index.
  1. International trade. 2. Commercial policy.
I. Krugman, Paul R. II. Title.
HF1379.H45   1989   382'.3   88-32609
ISBN 0-262-08182-2

A garden inclosed is my sister, my spouse;
a spring shut up, a fountain sealed.
Song of Sol. 4:12

Contents

Preface

The past decade has seen a major change in the theory of international trade. The traditional theory of trade based on comparative advantage has been complemented, and to some extent supplemented, by a new theoretical view in which increasing returns are a major independent source of trade. A world economy characterized by increasing returns will normally be one that is characterized by imperfect competition; thus the new approach to international trade has had as one of its key elements the integration of trade theory with industrial organization.

Now like any major change in theory, the rethinking of international trade was at first characterized by a proliferation of seemingly inconsistent models. While this proliferation is interesting and exciting, eventually it becomes important to take stock: to sort out the common elements among the profusion of alternative formulations, and to isolate the reasons for differences in results.

Four years ago we undertook to systematize and integrate the positive side of the new trade theory; that is, to present in a common framework as much as we could of the reasons why trade occurs and of its effects. The result of that effort was our book *Market Structure and Foreign Trade* (1985). Our feeling at that time was that the effort had been highly rewarding. The underlying commonality among different models was stronger, and the resulting framework greater in its reach, than we expected. The book has, we believe, also served a useful function as a core source for economists who wish to get an overview of the new developments in international trade.

In this book we endeavor to provide a similar service for the normative side of international trade. That is, we attempt here to systematize and present an overview of models of the effects of trade policy in imperfectly competitive markets. The aim is to provide a compact guide to the current state of thinking in this field. We hope that the resulting survey will be helpful both to researchers and to those who simply want to keep abreast of this dynamic area.

By its nature, a book like this one is for the most part not original. Nearly all of the main arguments presented here have their origin in the work of the major contributors to the policy application of the new international economics. These include Jagdish Bhagwati in the sixties, and James Brander, Avinash Dixit, Jonathan Eaton, Gene Grossman, Richard Harris, Barbara Spencer, and Anthony Venables in the eighties. Our own contribution, apart from the work of synthesis, is largely one of filling in a few gaps and offering as much of a unified approach as this diverse field allows.

Although the models of trade policy presented in this book are novel to those brought up in an older trade theory tradition, they are for the most part quite simple in their essential message. We have tried to take advantage of this underlying simplicity by pitching the bulk of the book at a relatively nontechnical level. Most of the book relies on verbal exposition, diagrams, and simple algebra; the more technical sections are indicated by asterisks. We envision this work as a useful handbook not only for researchers and graduate students but for advanced undergraduates and policymakers trained in economics.

We wish to thank Gene Grossman and a number of anonymous reviewers for comments on a preliminary draft. Most of the book was written when Helpman was a visiting professor at MIT.

Trade Policy and Market Structure

1   Introduction

Relatively few markets for industrial products and services meet the assumptions of perfect competition. Except in markets for a limited number of standardized commodities, firms do not usually view themselves as pure price-takers. Indeed, in many if not most markets there are only a limited number of important competitors, and these competitors are aware of the interdependence among their actions.

What is true of the economy as a whole is true of international trade as well. More than half of world trade is in manufactured goods, where markets are often oligopolistic rather than competitive. Markets for minerals are also often oligopolistic (or oligopsonistic, where the processing stage is highly concentrated). Even in agricultural products the pervasive roles of such institutions as marketing boards mean that the relevant players are not always price-takers. In other words, the study of international trade should be in part a study of international industrial organization.

Once stated, this observation seems obvious. Yet until a decade ago the theory of international trade was almost completely dominated by models in which perfect competition was assumed to prevail in all markets. This was true both of the positive theory of international trade—the explanation of why trade happens and what effect it has—and of the analysis of trade policy. With only a few exceptions, the international economist's toolbox contained models where all firms took prices as given and set their own prices equal to marginal cost.

Recently all this has changed. International trade theory has gone through a quiet but fundamental revolution in which a new approach has supplemented and, in some cases, supplanted the traditional analysis. The change began with a new theory of trade in which increasing returns played a coequal role with comparative advantage in giving rise to trade. Since increasing returns are normally inconsistent with perfect competition, this approach necessarily modeled markets as imperfectly competitive. Traditionally, trade theorists had avoided dealing with imperfect competition because they expected it to prove intractable and barren of useful insights. As work by a number of authors showed, however, this need not be the case; drawing on new developments in industrial organization theory, it proved possible to develop models of international trade in the presence of increasing returns and imperfect competition that rivaled orthodox models in their elegance and suggestiveness. Furthermore it became clear over time that what had at first appeared to be a proliferation of inconsistent models could be subsumed under a common framework that showed a fundamental commonality of concept. We can now talk with more or less justification of the theory of trade under increasing returns and imperfect competition as a coherent body of ideas. Indeed, this theory has now received widespread acceptance and has become part of the standard view.

Although the positive theory of trade under imperfect competition has now reached a certain maturity and acceptance, the same cannot be said of the theory of trade policy under imperfect competition. It is clear that changing one's view of why trade happens, and how international markets work, ought to change one's view of what kind of trade policy is appropriate. To oversimplify slightly, traditional competitive trade models provided support for free trade as part of the general case for the optimality of laissez-faire in a competitive economy. Allow that markets for traded goods and services are not typically perfectly competitive, and one opens the door for a variety of arguments for government intervention. That much is clear. But beyond this very little has been clear. As models of trade policy under imperfect competition have proliferated, the field has begun to take on some of the less attractive attributes of industrial organization theory. Instead of a convergence around some basic set of principles, there seems to be ever increasing diversity; cynics have been heard to remark that nowadays a bright graduate student can construct a model to yield any desired policy conclusion. Partly as a result, the policy implications of new trade theory have not received anything like the wide acceptance given to the descriptive side.

Our purpose in this book is to achieve some progress in this state of affairs by bringing at least some order to the variety of models that have appeared in the analysis of international trade policy in imperfectly competitive markets. In a previous book (Helpman and Krugman 1985) we offered a synthesis of the new positive theory of trade that we believe played a useful role both in solidifying the emerging consensus in that area and in communicating the developments to a wider audience of economists. What we would like to achieve here is the same thing for the policy side. Admittedly, the task is harder here. The analysis of trade policy under imperfect competition cannot be purged of all ambiguity and uncertainty because many of the conflicting results of different models are rooted in fundamental ambiguities in the underlying economics. The welfare effects of, say, a tariff levied against a foreign monopolist or any export subsidy to an oligopolistic industry are truly uncertain because they depend sensitively on market structure and aspects of behavior that cannot be determined a priori. What we can do, however, is isolate the main effects of trade policy in imperfectly competitive industries; where these effects conflict, we will at least know precisely where the source of uncertainty lies.

In presenting this analysis, we have chosen to focus narrowly on those issues in the analysis of trade policy that arise specifically from the prevalence of imperfect competition. This book is not a general treatise on trade policy. There is a huge and highly sophisticated literature that analyzes the implications for trade policy of external economies, of factor market distortions, of national (as opposed to individual) market power in trade, and so on. We briefly review some of the basic implications of this literature in chapter 2, but only as a backdrop. In reality trade policy for, say, the aircraft industry probably involves just about every consideration that has ever been mentioned, whether in traditional trade theory or its newer incarnation: externalities, wage differentials, national market power, non-economic objectives, rent seeking, tit-for-tat international rivalry, and oligopoly. We do not try to get it all in but focus on what is analytically new and different—namely, the role of imperfect competition.

Also through most of this book we rely on partial equilibrium models. This is a strategic decision. There are of course cases where general equilibrium effects could sharply alter conclusions; we point them out, and on occasion demonstrate them, where this seems necessary. For the most part, however, it seemed to us that at this point it was more important to present as concisely as possible an analysis of how trade policy works in particular markets than to invoke all the extra machinery needed to embed our analysis in a general equilibrium framework.

What, then, are the main themes in the economics of trade policy under imperfect competition? To some extent the themes are best expressed in terms of models rather than words, but it may be useful to state three basic issues that recur in much of the new trade literature, and in our book as well. These are the effects of trade policy on market power, the strategic effect of trade policy on competition, and the effect of trade policy on consumer choice.

1.1 Trade Policy and Market Power

The defining feature of imperfect competition is that firms do not take prices as given. As a result they do not regard the sole effect of selling another unit of output on their revenue as being the price of that unit; they have some conjecture about what effect selling more (or cutting their price in order to sell more) will have on the revenue they get from inframarginal sales. The end result is that price does not equal marginal cost, and normally exceeds it.

The ratio of price to marginal cost is one measure of market power. A distinctive feature of trade policy under imperfect competition—something that connot happen in perfectly competitive markets—is that a trade policy may alter the markup of price over marginal cost in ways that are either beneficial or harmful to the country that initiates the policy.

The most familiar argument here is that protection of domestic industries is anticompetitive, allowing domestic firms to increase their markups at the expense of domestic consumers. Economists have also long argued that the extent of this anticompetitive effect depends on the form of protection as well as its level. A tariff makes imports more costly, but they can still increase. A domestic industry that raises its prices too much will still find customers turning to imported substitutes. An import quota, on the other hand, prevents such substitution. Thus there is a familiar argument that quotas are in some sense more anticompetitive than tariffs (see Bhagwati 1965). At a formal level, however, this argument has been made only for the case of a pure monopolist confronted by import competition. In chapter 3 we review the argument that protection creates market power and that quotas are worse than tariffs, and we examine how well the argument holds up when the domestic industry is an oligopoly rather than a monopoly.

A more uncertain area is the effect of protection on the market power of foreign firms selling into the domestic market. An occasionally popular argument about tariffs is that they will be largely absorbed through a decline in foreign markups rather than passed on to consumers—"the foreigner pays the tariff." On the other hand, economists have often warned that import quotas simply cartelize foreign producers, inducing them to raise prices and actually benefiting foreigners at domestic expense. Chapter 4 treats both issues, asking in particular how the results depend on the market structure of the foreign industry.

A particularly interesting but problemataic question is how trade policy affects competition when both foreign and domestic suppliers are imperfectly competitive. On one side, such protection may in effect help domestic and foreign firms form a cartel, jointly exploiting domestic consumers. On the other hand, protection may serve as a strategic policy, of the kind discussed below, that shifts the game between foreign and domestic firms to the domestic firms' advantage. Or it may reallocate consumption in a socially desirable way from the point of view of the domestic country (also see below). These issues are treated in chapter 6.

Clearly, there are many issues involving the effects of trade policy on market power. One thread that ties them together is that of analytical method. What we show is that a surprisingly wide variety of problems involving market power can be analyzed by focusing on *perceived marginal revenue*—the increase in revenue that a firm expects to receive by producing one more unit, which is always less than the price (because of the effect on intramarginal sales) but may exceed the true marginal revenue that would prevail if the industry acted in concert. As we will see, a simple apparatus that compares the demand curve with the perceived and actual marginal revenue curves has applicability to many topics.

1.2 Strategic Effects

One of the most widely noticed and controversial aspects of the new literature on trade policy under imperfect competition is the possibility that interventionist trade policies may have beneficial "strategic" effects. A strategic move, as it is defined in modern industrial organization theory, is an action that is not profitable viewed in isolation but that alters the terms of subsequent competition to a firm's benefit. For example, a firm may invest in excess capacity that it does not intend to use, but whose presence deters potential competitors from entering the market. An implication of the new trade theory is that government trade policies may serve the same kind of role.

The now-famous example is the so-called Boeing-Airbus case (any resemblance to the real firms with those names may be purely coincidental). Suppose that there is an aircraft that either Boeing or Airbus could produce profitably but that—owing to the fixed costs of developing the plane—if both enter the market, both will lose money. Then there is a game of mutual deterrence between the firms in which each tries to convince the other that it is committed to produce; if it succeeds in making the commitment credible, a firm will deter its rival from entering and reap the profits. Firms may, however, lack any credible way to make a commitment to produce. In this situation government policy can make the difference. If European governments make a promise to pay Airbus a subsidy for production that is large enough to induce entry even if Boeing enters as well, then Boeing will find entry unprofitable and leave the field to Airbus. The result will be profits to Airbus that include not only the subsidy but also the profits from sole possession of the world market. Ignoring consumer costs, this will raise European national income at American expense (see Dixit and Kyle 1985).

Since it was first enunciated by Spencer and Brander (1983), the strategic trade policy argument has received wide attention. The Boeing-Airbus story seems at first sight to provide exactly the kind of argument for aggressive national trade policies that protectionists have always wanted, and it has been picked up in some variant in semipopular discussion. Yet from the start economists have been cautious. Does the strategic argument really offer a presumption in favor of aggressive policies or is this just a special case? Are there likely to be offsetting effects in the kind of industry to which the strategic trade argument might apply? How likely is it that a government will be able to have the information necessary to conduct a successful strategic policy?

In chapter 5 we offer a synthesis of the strategic trade policy debate as it has evolved over time. Interestingly, it is both possible and useful to apply to this debate the analytical method of contrasting perceived and actual marginal revenue; this helps us to offer a fairly compact and straightforward review of the main arguments. The basic result is to reinforce the skepticism about the general applicability of Boeing-Airbus type examples: on balance, the case for aggressive trade policies is relatively weak.

As we have noted, strategic issues also arise in the context of protection when both domestic and foreign firms have market power. Thus chapter 6, which studies such two-sided situations, also touches on strategic effects.

1.3 Production Efficiency

There is a quotation often attributed (we hope wrongly) to Abraham Lincoln, to the effect that when an American purchases a coat from a foreigner, the American gets the coat but the foreigner gets the money; when the coat is purchased from an American, the buyer still gets the coat but an American gets the money. The usual response of economists is that there is no such thing as a free coat: to make an all-American coat requires using resources that might more productively have been used to make something else (say, a Boeing).

Once one recognizes the importance of imperfect competition, the usual economist's response loses something of its force. Making a coat is costly, to be sure; but if its price exceeds marginal cost, then the resources used to make it might not have an equally productive use elsewhere. In principle, at least, policies that induce consumers to buy domestic goods whose price exceeds marginal cost may raise national income.

In this book we emphasize this theme in the context of intra-industry trade, where countries are exchanging goods in which neither has a comparative advantage. But we treat it also in other cases. We show that the argument has some validity. Perhaps even more surprising, protection can under some circumstances induce an increase in domestic production that actually lowers prices to consumers. However, the analysis also makes clear that this is not fundamentally an argument about trade policy, but rather one about how to handle the general problem of pricing under imperfect competition. When we turn to quantitative analysis of trade policy in chapter 8, it is notable that as more policy instruments are added the optimal policy typically looks less and less like a trade policy.

1.4 The Political Economy of the New Theory

This is a book about theory and methods, and not about policy. Yet one must realize that in economics theory will be used to advocate policy, whatever the theorist's intention. Strategic trade policy arguments have already appeared in support of views none of the concept's originators hold. So we need to say something here about the political economy of the theory we discuss.

Perhaps the most important point to make is that arguments based on imperfect competition are not the only or even perhaps the most powerful professionally respectable arguments against free trade. Arguments based, in particular, on external economies and factor market distortions are of long standing and have substantial empirical support. Thus the new theory should not be viewed as somehow shattering a monolithic view in which free trade was the only possible position (see, for example, Bhagwati 1971; Corden 1974).

Admittedly, there is a philosophical difference between the new arguments and the old. In traditional trade policy analysis, distortions that could justify government intervention were in effect superimposed on a theoretical structure whose basic logic was that of efficient, competitive equilibrium. In the new theory the imperfections are built into the structure from the beginning. So the arguments for interventionist policies are deeper in some logical sense. Yet in practical terms it is not clear how much difference this makes. One can imagine a competitive market without external economies, though one cannot imagine an oligopoly where price equals marginal cost. But the odds may be that external economies are a more important distortion of real-world economies than monopoly power.

Meanwhile there are a number of reasons for treating trade policy conclusions cautiously. One is uncertainty: as we show, the effects of a given policy may depend crucially on the details of the market. Another is domestic political economy: there are many people eager to appropriate the results of new trade theories to support highly dubious political causes, and international economists do not want to be apologists for crude protectionism. Finally, there is the problem of international rivalry: a policy that benefits one country acting unilaterally may be harmful if everyone does it. Since quantitative analyses seem to suggest that the gains from even optimal intervention are small (see chapter 8), many economists have suggested that free trade remains a useful rule of thumb, even though it is rarely optimal in modern trade models.

1.5 Organization

We develop the arguments gradually beginning with market structures that exhibit one-sided market power and proceeding to market structures that exhibit two-sided market power. After providing background on trade policy in competitive environments in chapter 2, in chapter 3 we discuss import protection by a country with a domestic monopoly or oligopoly. There we assume that foreign exporting firms are competitive, thereby isolating the role of domestic market power. In chapter 4 we deal with import protection of an economy that faces a foreign monopolist or a foreign oligopoly, while domestic supply is nonexistent or competitive. This market structure enables us to isolate the pure effects of foreign market power. In all of these chapters there are no strategic interactions.

We bring in strategic interactions in chapter 5; there we deal with export markets in which domestic firms with monopoly power compete with foreign firms with monopoly power. Our initial working hypothesis is that exportables are not used domestically. This way we need not worry about consumption effects, and we can isolate the pure effects of strategic interactions. At the end of the chapter we discuss domestic consumption. In chapter 6 we explore the role of strategic interactions in a domestic market in which domestic firms with market power compete with foreign firms that possess market power. This structure contains many elements of previous market structures as well as new ones. We concentrate on the latter.

Chapter 7 is devoted to trade policy in the presence of two-way trade. This may arise from monopolistic competition in differentiated products or for strategic reasons. In either case there are new features that bear on the effectiveness of trade policy. Finally, in chapter 8 we review the recent literature that tries to quantify the effects of trade policy in noncompetitive environments. We discuss the new methodology as well as the numerical results. In chapter 9 we sum up our findings and take stock of what has been learned.

References

Bhagwati, Jagdish N. (1965). "On the equivalence of tariffs and quotas." In Robert E. Baldwin et al. (eds.), *Trade, Growth and the Balance of Payments: Essays in Honor of Gottfried Haberler*. Chicago: Rand McNally.

Bhagwati, Jagdish N. (1971). "The generalized theory of distortions and welfare." In Jagdish N. Bhagwati et al. (eds.), *Trade, Balance of Payments, and Growth: Papers in International Economics in Honor of Charles P. Kindleberger*. Amsterdam: North-Holland.

Corden, Max W. (1974). *Trade Policy and Economic Welfare*. Oxford: Clarendon Press.

Dixit, Avinash, and Kyle, A. S. (1985). "The use of protection and subsidies for entry promotion and deterrence." *American Economic Review* 75: 139–152.

Helpman, Elhanan, and Krugman, Paul R. (1985). *Market Structure and Foreign Trade*. Cambridge, MA: MIT Press.

Spencer, Barbara, and Brander, James (1983). "International R&D rivalry and industrial strategy." *Review of Economic Studies* 50: 707–722.

2 Trade Policy under Perfect Competition

Although this book is concerned with the theory of trade policy in imperfectly competitive markets, it is useful to begin with a brief exposition of some main results from the theory of trade policy under conditions of perfect competition. For one thing, this traditional theory is important as a backdrop, to help us see what is new about the results presented later (and equally important, what is not). Also a presentation of traditional theory can serve as a convenient place to introduce some concepts and techniques that will recur in our later analysis.

The version of traditional theory we present in this chapter is of course highly abbreviated—there is an enormous literature on trade policy under perfect competition, too large to do justice in a single chapter. In particular, we will focus primarily on a partial equilibrium model of a single market, thereby neglecting important general equilibrium issues. Also this chapter is in no sense a literature survey—too many people have contributed to the vast edifice that is traditional trade theory even to start giving credit where credit is due. We note simply that a more extensive survey in the same spirit as that of this chapter may be found in Corden (1974), that a modern textbook treatment that follows a similar approach may be found in Krugman and Obstfeld (1988), and that some of the more subtle issues in trade policy analysis are treated in Dixit and Norman (1980) and Woodland (1982).

In this chapter, then, we briefly review the analysis of trade policies in a competitive market. We begin by considering three basic trade policies: tariffs, import quotas, and export subsidies/taxes. We then turn to the calculation of optimal policies, with a brief digression into general equilibrium considerations, and follow this with a discussion of the case for government intervention in competitive markets. We conclude with some welfare algebra that will find repeated use in later chapters.

2.1 Tariff Analysis

Figure 2.1 illustrates the determination of trade volume and prices in a single competitive market. The quantity m represents the imports of a country that we will call Home, and also the exports of a country that we will call Foreign. The curve D represents Home's *import demand curve*; it shows the excess of domestic demand over supply at each price. The curve S^* represents Foreign's *export supply curve*, defined by the excess of domestic supply over demand at each price.

In the absence of any tariff or transportation cost, equilibrium will occur at point 1, where the two curves cross. At the price p_F Home's excess demand is m_F, and so is Foreign's excess supply; thus for the world as a whole excess demand is zero.

Now consider imposing a tariff. In a perfectly competitive market it does not matter whether the tariff is a specific tariff per physical unit or an ad valorem tariff levied as a proportion of the price, so we will simplify by assuming a specific tariff at a rate t. The effect of such a tax must be to drive a wedge between the price of the good in Foreign and in Home. In figure 2.1 the tariff is shown as raising the internal price in Home to p_t, while lowering the price in Foreign to p_t^*. The difference $p_t - p_t^*$ must just equal the tariff rate t.

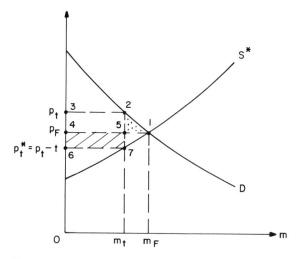

Figure 2.1

Clearly, the tariff makes producers and the government in Home better off, and Home consumers worse off. To say more than this, it is necessary to make some further assumptions. The standard assumptions are the following. First, we assume that income distribution is not an issue: a marginal dollar of government revenue has the same social value as a marginal dollar of producer or consumer surplus. Second, we assume that the economy is efficient in all markets other than this one, so that consumer surplus and producer surplus are accurate measures of welfare. The first assumption may be defended either by the assertion that the government manages income distribution using some other tools or simply as a working assumption that puts distributional issues on one side. The second assumption will be relaxed in section 2.6.

Given these assumptions, the welfare effects of the tariff can be measured by the effects on consumer plus producer surplus together with government revenue. In Home, the combined effect on consumer and producer surplus may be represented by the reduction in the area under the import demand curve; that is, by the area 12345 in figure 2.1. Meanwhile, the tariff generates revenue equal to the tariff rate multiplied by the post-tariff volume of imports, that is, the area 2367.

The overall welfare effect is the difference between these two. Netting out the area of overlap, we have a loss represented by the dot-shaded triangle 125, and a gain represented by the line-shaded rectangle 4576. The loss may be regarded as a distortion loss due to the wedge introduced between supply and demand. The gain may be regarded as a terms of trade effect. To see the latter point, notice that if Home were a small country, unable to affect its terms of trade, it would face an import supply curve S^* that was horizontal. In that case the area 4576 would vanish, and the distortion loss would be all that was left.

An important point is also clear from the figure: some sufficiently small tariff always raises welfare. Imagine making the tariff rate progressively smaller. Then it is obvious from the geometry that the loss will get small faster than the gain; more formally, the loss is second order in the tariff, while the gain is first order. So a small enough tariff is always welfare improving. For large tariffs, of course, there is a trade-off between the distortion loss and the terms of trade gain; by analyzing this trade-off, we will arrive at the formula for an optimal tariff derived later in this chapter.

2.2 Import Quotas

Suppose that instead of imposing a tariff, the Home government had imposed a quota on imports, limiting them to m_t. To enforce this limit, the right to import would have to be limited to those who receive licenses. What should be immediately clear is that this will have the same effect in increasing internal prices that a tariff would; the only difference is that what would have been tariff revenue accrues to the recipients of the licenses instead.

Returning to figure 2.1, if an import quota of m_t is imposed, the effect must be to raise the internal price in Home to p_t. The owner of a license to import a unit of the good can then purchase the good at the price p_t^* and sell it at the price p_t, collecting as her rent the tariff-equivalent t. Thus the overall rents received by recipients of licenses will be the same as the revenue generated by a tariff that limited imports to the same quantity.

Although the price and output effects of a quota and a tariff are equivalent in competitive markets, the welfare effects depend crucially on how import licenses are distributed. One possibility would be an auction of import rights by the Home government. In this case the price of an import license would absorb the rent, and the revenue from the auction would be the same as the revenue from the equivalent tariff. A second possibility would be assignment of import rights to Home residents (as in the case of Japanese citrus fruit quotas). In this case domestic residents rather than the country would receive the rents. In either of these cases the overall welfare impact would be the same as in the case of a tariff (as long as we continue to ignore domestic income distribution).

A third possibility, however, is that the licenses are assigned to foreigners—as in the case of U.S. sugar quotas, or any of the proliferating "voluntary" restraints of modern protectionism. In this case the foreigners get the rents, and the consumer plus producer loss 12345 is uncompensated by any revenue gain. Thus an import quota whose licenses are assigned to foreigners produces an unambiguous loss to the protecting country. A major puzzle for the political economy of trade policy is to explain why such a seemingly self-punishing policy should have become the protectionist measure of choice in the last two decades.

2.3 Export Subsidies and Taxes

We turn next to trade policies pursued by the exporting nation in an industry. In figures 2.2 and 2.3, X represents Home's exports, which are also Foreign's imports. The curve S is now Home's export supply curve, and D^* is Foreign's import demand curve.

In popular discussions of trade policy, tariffs are usually lumped together with export subsidies, since both seem to favor domestic producers over foreign. The welfare effects of a tariff and an export subsidy are, however, quite different even in a competitive market. Figure 2.2 shows the effects of an export subsidy of s per unit. The subsidy raises the internal price in Home to p_s, while lowering the price abroad to p_s^*; the difference between these prices is of course equal to the subsidy rate.

Home producers gain while consumers lose, with the net change in consumer plus producer surplus measured by 1234. Exports rise from X_F to X_s, implying a subsidy bill equal to the area of the rectangle 2356. What is immediately clear is that the subsidy is unambiguously larger than the benefits. Netting out offsetting areas, the loss has two components: the dot-shaded triangle 127, which may be interpreted as a distortion loss, and the line-shaded rectangle 4567, which may be interpreted as a terms of trade loss. For the difference be-

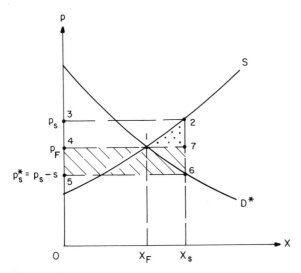

Figure 2.2

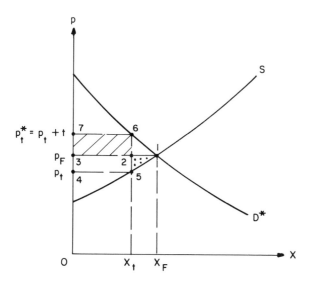

Figure 2.3

tween a tariff and an export subsidy is, of course, that the former improves the terms of trade while the latter worsens them.

Clearly, the possibility of a welfare-improving policy on the export side must lie on the other side, in an export *tax*. Figure 2.3 illustrates the effects of a tax levied at the rate t. The internal price of exports in Home falls to p_t, reducing the sum of consumer plus producer surplus by the area 12345. However, the tax yields revenue equal to aftertax export volume multiplied by the tax rate, or the area of the rectangle 4567. Netting out offsetting areas, the result is a distortion loss equal to the area of the dot-shaded triangle 125, set against a terms-of-trade gain equal to the area of the line-shaded rectangle 2376. As in the case of a tariff, we can see that a sufficiently small export tax is always welfare improving.

An interesting point to note is that if Foreign were to impose an import quota and assign the licenses to residents of Home, the effect would be the same as that of an export tax imposed by Home. Thus certain kinds of protectionism can actually benefit the exporting nation at the importer's expense.

Again, given the results here, the political economy of trade in the real world is somewhat puzzling. Small export taxes should normally be beneficial, whereas export subsidies should always be harmful. In reality export subsidies are common, but export taxes are rare.

2.4 Optimal Trade Taxes

We have seen that sufficiently small taxes on trade, either on imports or on exports, will increase the taxing nation's welfare. As the tax rate is increased, however, the losses cease to be second order so that at some point the costs of a further tax increase outweigh the benefits. One way to think about the optimal tax is that it is set by raising the tax rate to the point where the gain from improved terms of trade is just offset by the loss from further aggravating the distortion due to the tax wedge.

A useful alternative way to look at this problem, however, is illustrated in figure 2.4 for the case of an export tax. To maximize welfare, an exporting country wants to make the marginal social cost of a good equal to its marginal social value in all uses. To export an additional unit of a good, a country must either cut its consumption or increase its production; the social cost of either is measured by the domestic price, and so social marginal cost of exports is in fact measured by the export supply curve. The social return from an additional unit of exports, however, is measured not by the price of the export but by the marginal revenue from that export. Thus we need to draw in a marginal revenue schedule for exports, which lies below the Foreign export demand curve because exporting more depresses the price of inframarginal units. The optimal level of ex-

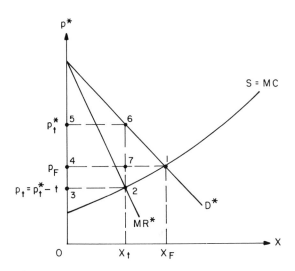

Figure 2.4

ports is where export supply intersects the marginal revenue rather than the demand curve, at point 2 rather than point 1.

The optimal export tax reduces the internal price of exports to the marginal revenue from exporting. Suppose that we write the demand for Home's exports in inverse form as $p^* = p^*(X)$. Then the revenue from exports equals $Xp^*(X)$, and the marginal revenue is $p^*(X) + X[dp^*(X)/dX]$. This may be rewritten as $p^*(X)[1 + (X/p^*(X))(dp^*(X)/dX)]$, or

$$MR^* = p^*(X) \left[1 - \frac{1}{\epsilon^*} \right],$$

where ϵ^* is the elasticity of foreign demand for Home exports.

Now suppose that we want to impose a tax that makes p, the internal price in Home, equal to this marginal revenue. Here it is most convenient to think in terms of an ad valorem tax at a rate τ. Then we know that $p = p^*/(1 + \tau)$. If we want to set $p = MR^*$, we must therefore have

$$\tau_{\text{exp}} = \frac{1}{\epsilon^* - 1} \tag{2.1}$$

as the formula for the optimal export tax.

To calculate the optimal import tariff, we note that the true cost of an additional unit of imports is not its price, but its price plus the effect of purchasing an additional unit on the cost of inframarginal units. Thus, if the import supply curve can be written $p^*(m)$, the marginal cost of imports is $p^*(m) + m[dp^*(m)/dm]$. The marginal import cost curve is shown as MC_m in figure 2.5. The optimal tariff sets the internal price equal to this marginal cost.

As in the case of the optimal export tax, the optimal tariff may be expressed in terms of the elasticity of the foreign supply curve. Setting marginal import cost equal to domestic price and rearranging, we find the optimal tariff to be

$$\tau_{\text{imp}} = \frac{1}{\zeta^*}, \tag{2.2}$$

where ζ^* is the elasticity of foreign supply.

Comparing both these formulas, we note that in each case the optimal rate is lower, the more elastic the relevant foreign curve; that is, the less effect Home can have on its terms of trade. In the limiting

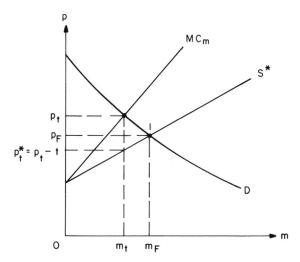

Figure 2.5

case where Home is a small country unable to affect its terms of trade at all, we have $\epsilon^* = \zeta^*$ equal to infinity, and free trade is the optimal policy.

2.5 A Note on General Equilibrium

In describing the effects of trade policies, we have made the partial equilibrium assumption that supply and demand in each market depend only on the policies undertaken in that market. In general equilibrium, however, this cannot always be true. In particular, when the values of exports and imports must be equal, an import tariff must necessarily affect exports and an export tax affect imports.

Consider a country that exports a single good and imports some other good. Let the price of its exportable relative to the price of its importable be P. Then the budget constraint requires that the export supply and import demand functions be related by

$$PX^*(P) \equiv m^*(P).$$

Given this, the elasticities of export supply and import demand must also be related by

$$1 + \zeta^* = \epsilon^*.$$

But this implies, from (2.1) and (2.2), that the optimal import and export tax rates of a country that trades with this country are equal:

$$\tau_{\text{exp}} = \tau_{\text{imp}} = \frac{1}{\epsilon^* - 1} = \frac{1}{\zeta^*} . \qquad (2.3)$$

This equality reflects a deeper point, the equivalence of tariffs and export taxes (see Lerner 1936). In general equilibrium an across-the-board tax on exports has the same effect as one on imports, and thus it should come as no surprise that the optimal tax rate is the same in either case.

2.6 Domestic Distortions and Trade Policy

The case for government intervention in trade, as we have presented it so far, depends entirely on the possibility that taxes on trade can improve the terms of trade and thus benefit a country at its trading partners' expense. The bulk of theoretical analysis of trade policy, however, is concerned with other possibilities of gains from intervention, arising from violations of the assumption that consumer and producer surplus accurately measure social costs and benefits. The general approach to trade policy may be described as the theory of *domestic distortions*: trade policy may be useful because it helps to offset some malfunctioning of markets.

A great many kinds of potential domestic distortions have been studied, but two main types are most commonly cited. First are imperfections in factor markets. These include differentials in wages among industries, unemployment, rationing in capital markets, and so on. Second are external economies: technological spillovers between firms, learning effects, and negative externalities such as pollution. Either of these kinds of market failure can cause private and social cost to differ, providing a justification for government action.

The essence of the domestic distortion argument is illustrated in figure 2.6. This portays a single industry in a country that is assumed to be small, facing a given world price p^*. The industry's domestic suppy curve, which is also its private marginal cost curve, is indicated by S; its domestic demand curve by D.

We also indicate a social marginal cost curve, shown as SMC. This is drawn lying below the supply curve: social marginal cost in this industry is assumed smaller than private. This might be because the industry employs workers who would otherwise be unemployed or because it generates valuable externalities, or any of a variety of reasons; whatever the reason, we suppose that such a divergence between social and private cost exists and can be identified.

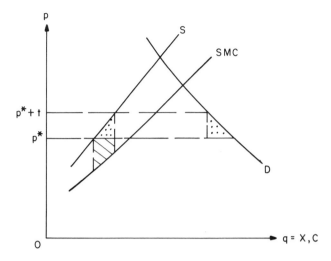

Figure 2.6

Now consider the effects of a tariff t. In a small country a tariff does not lower foreign prices, and thus raises domestic prices by the full amount of the tariff. If social and private costs were the same, the tariff would unambiguously reduce welfare; by calculating the effects on revenue and on consumer and producer surplus, one finds that the net loss is measured by the two dot-shaded triangles (which measure the production and consumption losses, respectively).

However, given the domestic distortion, there is now an offsetting gain. A unit of domestic production replaces a unit of imports, worth p^*, but the social cost of producing that extra unit is measured by the SMC curve, which by assumption lies below the world price under free trade. Thus the apparent production loss should net out a production gain, represented by the line-shaded area.

By reasoning that by now should be familiar, we can see that for a small enough tariff the gains will exceed the losses, so that the divergence between private and social marginal cost offers a justification for some degree of protection. This is an important point. The arguments for trade intervention that will be presented in this book are by no means the only possible justifications for deviating from free trade.

Figure 2.6 can also be used to make another important point: a tariff is at most a second-best policy. To see this, notice that a production subsidy at the rate t would achieve the same level of output, and thus the same production gain, as the tariff indicated. Yet it would avoid causing the consumption distortion that generates off-setting losses. Thus there exists a production subsidy that is better than a tariff. A more sophisticated view would note that the extra social benefits of production rarely come from the productive activity per se but come from some particular activity associated with pro-duction, such as the employment of otherwise unemployed labor or the generation of knowledge. A policy that directly encourages these desirable activities can do better than a production subsidy, and a fortiori better than a tariff.

The domestic distortions case for a tariff, then, is really a case for a domestic rather than a trade policy. If for some reason only trade policies are available, they can be beneficial, but they are blunt in-struments for the purpose. As we will see particularly in chapters 7 and 8, the same is often true of the imperfect competition case for government intervention: it is not really a case for trade policy per se.

2.7* Algebra for Small Policy Changes

Occasional arguments in the following chapters require formulas for the evaluation of small changes in prices and quantities. For this reason this section develops the suitable equations. We begin with general formulas that do not depend on market structure, show their implications for competitive economies, and briefly discuss how they can be applied to other market structures.[1]

We treat the private sector as a representative individual, whose welfare level can be measured by means of an indirect utility function $v(p_C, I)$, where I denotes income and p_C denotes the *vector* of con-sumer prices. The government may collect taxes or provide subsidies to consumption and production; we will not deal with input taxes. A tariff is treated as a tax on domestic consumption and subsidy to domestic production. Similarly, an export subsidy is treated as a subsidy to domestic production and tax on domestic consumption. This particular way of viewing trade taxes simplifies notation.

We assume that the government maintains a balanced budget. Moreover the excess of tax revenue over subsidies is rebated to the

---

1. Readers who are not familiar with the type of calculations employed in this section can find more details in Dixit and Norman (1980) or Woodland (1982).

private sector in a lump-sum fashion. By the same token the government raises lump-sum taxes whenever subsidies exceed ordinary taxes. This specification allows us to represent private sector income as

$$I = p \cdot X + (p_C - p^*) \cdot C + (p^* - p) \cdot X,$$

where p denotes the vector of domestic producer prices, p^* denotes the vector of foreign prices, X denotes the vector of domestic production, and C denotes the vector of domestic consumption. The first term on the right-hand side represents production income. This is disbursed to the private sector in the forms of rewards to factor inputs or pure profits. The second term represents the lump-sum rebate of consumption taxes, and the third term represents the lump-sum rebate of production taxes.

To see how tariffs fit into this formulation, suppose that good i is imported and pays a specific tariff t_i. Then $p_i = p_{Ci} = p_i^* + t_i$, and the ith component of the last two terms reduces to $t_i(C_i - X_i)$, which equals tariff revenue on good i. Export subsidies have a similar representation.

We measure welfare changes by means of $dU = dv/v_I$, namely, by the change in utility divided by the marginal utility of income. Using the standard properties of the indirect utility function and the definition of income we gave earlier, we obtain the following representation of the welfare change:

$$dU = -m \cdot dp^* + p^* \cdot dX + (p_C - p^*) \cdot dC, \tag{2.4}$$

where $m = C - X$ denotes the vector of imports (an imported good has a positive sign, whereas an exported good has a negative sign). The first term on the right-hand side represents the gain from improved terms of trade: an increase in the foreign price of an exportable raises welfare, but an increase in the foreign price of an importable reduces welfare. The second term represents the gain from an improved production composition. A change in the composition of production that raises its value in terms of foreign prices (the suitable shadow prices for cost-benefit analysis) raises welfare. The last term represents the consumption-wedge effect. For small taxes, the consumption-wedge effect is second order in size and can be disregarded.

Formula (2.4) is quite general; it applies to both competitive and noncompetitive market structures. It can be modified in various ways to suit particular circumstances. For example, let production be efficient; namely, let the economy be on its transformation surface. Then, if c denotes the vector of marginal costs (proportional to the gradient of the transformation surface), $c \cdot dX = 0$, and (2.4) can be rewritten as

$$dU = -m \cdot dp^* + (p^* - c) \cdot dX + (p_C - p^*) \cdot dC. \tag{2.5}$$

There are many forms of noncompetitive market structures in which production efficiency is attained and for which this formula can be applied. For example, (2.5) applies in situations in which oligopolies produce with constant returns to scale and entry is restricted by government regulation. In fact, this formula also applies to situations in which the oligopolists produce with increasing returns to scale and there are fixed entry costs, as long as we deal with small changes that do *not* lead to changes in the number of firms (because in this case $c \cdot dX = 0$ applies). It is, however, necessary to use (2.4) directly whenever there are economies of scale and the number of firms changes (see, for example, chapter 5).

The second term on the right-hand side of (2.5) represents another form of the efficiency gain from changes in the composition of production. The changing composition of production raises income and welfare when the economy expands production of goods whose foreign price exceeds domestic marginal production costs, and it reduces income and welfare when the economy expands production of goods whose foreign price is below domestic marginal production costs.

The next thing to note is that when all taxes and subsidies are on trade, $p = p_C = p^* + t$ and (2.5) can be rewritten as

$$dU = -m \cdot dp^* + t \cdot dm + (p - c) \cdot dX. \tag{2.6}$$

The first two terms are standard; the terms of trade and the tax-wedge effects (see the lined and dotted areas, respectively, in figure 2.1). The last term equals zero in competitive economies with marginal cost pricing. In noncompetitive economies, however, the last term plays an important role. It shows that efficiency in the composition of output is gained when industries that mark up prices over marginal costs expand and efficiency in the composition of output is lost when these industries contract.

These formulas for the decomposition of welfare changes can be used to evaluate trade and other policies, as we will repeatedly demonstrate in the following chapters.

References

Corden, W. Max (1974). *Trade Policy and Economic Welfare*. Oxford: Clarendon Press.

Dixit, Avinash and Norman, Victor (1980). *Theory of International Trade*. Cambridge: Cambridge University Press.

Krugman, Paul R., and Obstfeld, Maurice (1988). *International Economics: Theory and Policy*. Chicago: Scott Foresman.

Lerner, Abba (1936). "The symmetry between import and export taxes." *Economica* 3: 306–313.

Woodland, Allan D. (1982). *International Trade and Resource Allocation*. Amsterdam: North-Holland.

3   Protection and Domestic
        Market Power

We begin our analysis of the effects of trade policy in an imperfectly competitive world with the oldest insight in this area. This is the idea that international trade increases competition and thus, conversely, that protection creates domestic monopoly. This idea goes back to Adam Smith, and it has long been one of the reasons that economists give for believing that the gains from trade and the costs of protection are larger than their own models seem to suggest. Bhagwati (1965) added a further idea: that different *types* of protection varied in their effects on monopoly power; in particular, that quantitative restrictions such as import quotas are worse than tariffs. This is an idea that has gone beyond mere theoretical speculation to inform policy decisions.

To isolate the role of protection in affecting domestic competition, in this chapter we examine a series of models in which an imperfectly competitive domestic industry faces competitively supplied imports. This is of course not always realistic; if a domestic industry is an oligopoly, it will often be the case that the same is true of the industry in the rest of the world. This case does, however, have the virtue of isolating the issue of domestic market power. We turn to the issues of foreign market power, and the competition between firms from different countries, all of whom have market power, in later chapters.

3.1 The Case of an Import-Competing Monopolist

We begin our analysis of the effects of trade policy on domestic market power with a case that in its simplicity and clear policy moral has become canonical. This is the case of a single domestic firm whose monopoly power is limited by actual or potential competition from imports. The conclusions that we derive from studying this case essentially define the questions we will be asking in the rest of this chapter. The simplest model of an import-competing monopolist is one in which protection creates market power where none would otherwise exist, and import quotas create more market power than tariffs. The remainder of the chapter will be largely concerned with testing the robustness of these conclusions to more complex and realistic formulations of the market structure of the import-competing industry.

The simplest version of the model can be conveyed diagrammatically (see Bhagwati 1965 for the original argument). In figure 3.1 we show a domestic firm with upward-sloping marginal cost curve MC (the consequences of a downward sloping marginal cost are considered later). The *domestic* demand for the firm's output is represented by D. Corresponding to the demand curve D is a marginal revenue curve MR. The firm is not free to choose a profit-maximizing price along MR, however, because it faces the threat of competition from imports, which we assume are perfect substitutes for the firm's output and are available in perfectly elastic supply at a world price p_W. We assume also that there is no possibility of export.

In the absence of import competition, the firm would like to move to the profit-maximizing price p_M and the corresponding level of output X_M. However, under free trade it will be unable to do this. Indeed, at any price above p_W imports will undercut the firm, so p_W represents an upper bound on the firm's price. In the absence of

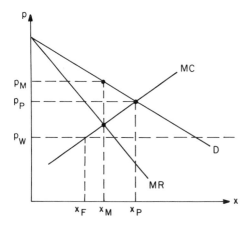

Figure 3.1

protection, then, the firm clearly will charge the price p_W. Its profit-maximizing output decision will be to produce up to the point where this externally dictated price equals marginal cost, that is, to behave as if it were a perfect competitor, and output will therefore equal X_F. Under free trade, then, this is a monopolist with no monopoly power.

Effects of a Tariff

Now suppose that the monopolist is protected by an import tariff. It makes no difference in this case whether the tariff is specific or ad valorem, so let us assume for simplicity that it is specific. Then the price at which imports are available is the world price plus the tariff, $p_W + t$.

The effect of the tariff on the output and price of the domestic firm depends on how large the tariff is. It is useful to define p_P as the price at which the tariff is just prohibitive, that is, chokes off all imports; this price is defined by the point where the MC and D curves cross, as indicated in figure 3.1. Then the tariff's effect depends on whether it is small so that $p_W + t < p_P$; medium-sized so that $p_P < p_W + t < p_M$; or large so that $p_M < p_W + t$.

If the tariff is small the firm's basic position is the same as under free trade—that is, its price is constrained by the price of competing imports, and it sets output where this externally dictated price equals marginal cost. The effect of tariffs in this range on the firm's price and output is therefore exactly the same as it would be in a perfectly competitive industry with the marginal cost curve MC. The higher the tariff within this range, the higher are both the output and price of the firm.

If the tariff is in the range where $p_P < p_W + t < p_M$, the price of potentially competing imports still constrains the firm from charging the monopoly price. However, the firm can no longer set output where marginal cost equals the tariff-inclusive import price, since this would involve producing more than domestic consumers want to buy at that price. Instead, the profit-maximizing strategy is clearly to set the price equal to $p_W + t$ but to produce only as much as is demanded domestically at that price. Two points should be noted about this outcome. First, in this case there are no actual imports. It is the *threat* of imports, rather than actual import penetration, that limits the price the monopolist can charge. Second, it is clear that increases in the tariff within this range have a perverse effect on output. If the tariff is increased, the firm will be free to increase its price. But since domestic consumers will demand less at the higher price, the firm will reduce its output.

Finally, at a tariff so high that $p_W + t > p_M$, the price of competing imports will cease to be binding on the firm. The firm is free to charge its profit-maximizing monopoly price, and changes in the tariff rate within this range will have no effects.

This three-part analysis may be usefully summarized by figure 3.2, which shows how the domestic firm's output varies with the tariff-inclusive price of competing imports. For low tariffs, the firm matches tariff increases with its own price increases and slides up its marginal cost curve. For tariff increases beyond the prohibitive level, the domestic price continues to rise one for one, but the firm now slides back along the domestic demand curve. Finally, at sufficiently high tariffs domestic price and output remain unchanged at the closed-economy monopoly levels.

Effects of an Import Quota

Figure 3.3 shows the effects of a quota that limits imports to some maximum quantity $\bar{m}$. If the domestic firm charges a price below p_W, this limitation will not be binding, since there will be no incentive to import. For any price above p_W, however, $\bar{m}$ units will be imported, and the domestic firm will satisfy the residual demand. The result will therefore be to present the domestic firm with a new demand

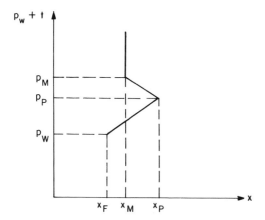

Figure 3.2

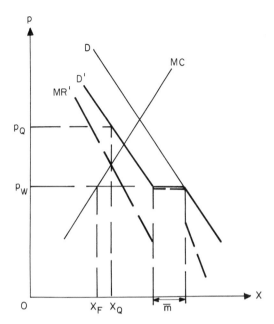

Figure 3.3

curve D' that has three segments (represented in the figure by the heavy lines): for prices above p_W, it is the domestic market demand shifted left by the quota amount $\overline{m}$; for prices below p_W, it is the total domestic market demand; and there is a horizontal segment at p_W. Corresponding to the new demand curve is a new marginal revenue curve MR' (represented by the broken lines), also with the three segments. (Note that at the horizontal segment marginal revenue and the demand curve coincide.) In situations where the country would have imported the good under free trade, the rightmost segment of MR' is never relevant, so we drop it in later diagrams.

In the situation illustrated in figure 3.3, the quota is set at a level smaller than the free trade level of imports. The domestic firm maximizes profits by choosing the level of output where marginal cost equals this new marginal revenue, shown in the figure as X_Q with the corresponding price p_Q.

An import quota may, however, still have an effect even when it is set larger than the free trade import level. This case is illustrated in figure 3.4. It is immediately apparent that in this case the marginal cost curve crosses the marginal revenue curve in two places—that is,

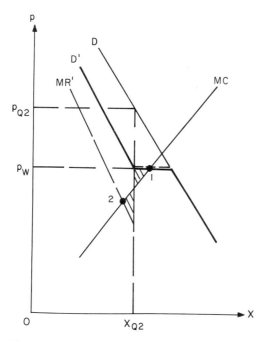

Figure 3.4

there are two *locally* profit-maximizing levels of output. One of these, at point 1, is the free trade output; the other, at point 2, is a position in which the monopolist takes advantage of the quota to reduce output and raise the price above its free trade level.

To determine which of these is the *global* profit maximum, consider the thought experiment of gradually reducing output from point 1 to point 2. At first, marginal revenue exceeds marginal cost. Thus in reducing output to the level X_{Q2} at which the quota becomes binding, the firm will reduce profits by an amount that is measured by the shaded triangle with a vertex at point 1. As output is further reduced, however, marginal revenue is less than marginal cost, and so the fall in output to the monopoly level produces a rise in profits, measured by the area of the shaded triangle with a vertex at point 2. The decision on whether to produce at the free trade level or retreat inside the quota therefore depends on which of these triangles is larger.

What is immediately clear is that when the quota exceeds the free trade import level, the more restrictive it is (the closer it is to the free trade level of imports), the more likely it is that the firm will choose to reduce its output. In particular, a quota that limits imports to precisely their free trade level (which would not be binding under perfect competition) will definitely lead to a reduction in output and a rise in the price.

There is no correspondence in the case of an import quota to the case of a tariff that raises price without creating monopoly power. Any binding quota will have the effect of leading the firm to behave in a monopolistic fashion.

Comparing Quotas and Tariffs

We can now turn to the most famous result of this analysis: that a tariff and an import quota that lead to the same level of imports have differing effects, with the quota leading to a higher domestic price and a lower domestic output than the "equivalent" tariff.[1]

This may be seen immediately for the comparison of prohibitive tariffs with a total ban on imports. As we have seen earlier, there is a range of tariffs for which imports are zero, but for which the domestic price is below p_M and the domestic output larger than X_M. On the other hand, a quantitative restriction that eliminates imports will immediately leave the domestic firm free to move to the monopoly price and output. The point is of course that in the range where $p_W + t < p_M$, the threat of imports constrains the domestic price, even though there are no imports in fact; an import quota eliminates this threat, creating more market power and thus a higher domestic price.

The same is true when positive levels of imports are allowed, as figure 3.5 shows. The technique used is to construct an import quota that limits imports to the same level as an arbitrary tariff. We first find the level of imports corresponding to some nonprohibitive tariff and then compare its effects with a quota set at the same level of imports. The postquota demand curve D' facing the firm passes through the tariff production/price point 1. Its corresponding marginal revenue curve therefore lies below, leading to a quota equilib-

---

1. The import level does not provide the single logical criterion of comparison. But we need a clear criterion in order to set the two instruments on the same footing. Comparisons of tariffs and quotas that achieve the same domestic output of the protected industry can also be found in the literature. The results are sensitive to the choice of criterion.

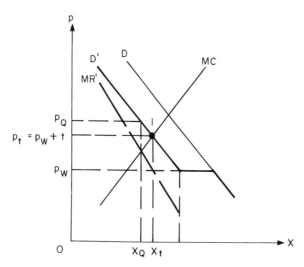

Figure 3.5.

rium with a lower output X_Q and a higher price p_Q. This stems from the fact that the tariff-constrained demand curve is more elastic than the quota-constrained demand curve for output X_t.

A special case of this result is where the tariff to which we find a quota equivalent is zero—that is, where imports are restricted only not to exceed their free trade level. Clearly, the result is a rise in the price and a fall in the output of the protected firm.

This example also shows that the effect of an import quota on domestic output may be perverse. Here limiting imports leads to a fall in domestic output, instead of the rise that would occur under perfect competition. The reason is of course that the import quota creates monopoly power that is used to restrict output and raise the price.

The moral of this story is therefore clear: an import quota creates more domestic monopoly power than a tariff that restricts imports by the same amount, and it therefore leads both to lower domestic output and a higher domestic price. Although both the tariff and the quota reduce welfare in this model, the quota obviously reduces it more.

How robust are these conclusions? We first consider some extensions of the case of a domestic monopolist, then turn to more complex market structures.

Declining Marginal Costs

The basic model assumes upward-sloping marginal cost in order to yield an interior solution. However, the existence of a domestic monopolist may result from the presence of some kind of increasing returns. Although increasing returns may be consistent with upward-sloping marginal cost, this certainly suggests the real possibility of downward-sloping costs. We consider the case of declining marginal cost next.

The most important effect of downward-sloping marginal cost is to introduce a discontinuity in the response of output to the tariff rate. Figure 3.6 illustrates the point. AC represents the firm's average cost, and MC its marginal cost. As drawn, at the free trade price the firm is unable to operate profitably in the domestic market; if it were to match the price of imports and fill all domestic demand, its average cost would still be above p_W.[2] (If this were not the case, there would be no imports in the first place, as will be clear in a moment.) A tariff of t_S is needed to bring the firm into production—but as soon as this tariff is provided, the firm produces a large positive output X_S and

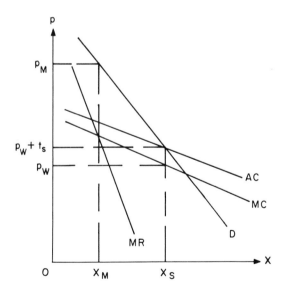

Figure 3.6

2. If the firm could export, it might be able to export profitably; we assume that it cannot.

displaces all imports (see Corden 1974, ch. 8). Any further increase in the tariff above this "scientific" level will allow the firm to increase its price and reduce its output until the monopoly position is reached. With downward-sloping marginal cost, then, the upward-sloping section of the curve in figure 3.2 is eliminated.

The nonequivalence of tariffs and quotas clearly remains. As in the case of upward-sloping marginal cost, there is a range of prohibitive tariffs that raise prices less and lead to higher output than a simple prohibition of imports. For less restrictive import quotas, there are no equivalent tariffs, since tariffs either eliminate imports or fail to establish the domestic industry. Nevertheless, the basic message about the role of protection in creating market power and the greater monopolizing effect of quotas seems to come through essentially intact.

Imperfect Substitutes

We now consider the case of a domestic monopolist that faces competitively supplied imports that are imperfect substitutes for its own production. When imports are not a perfect substitute for domestic production, the single domestic firm has some monopoly power even under free trade; thus protection can no longer have the effect of creating monopoly power when none existed before. However, the monopoly power of the firm may still be increased by protection. We want to see whether it continues to be true that quotas are protective to a greater extent than tariffs.

Consider, then, a firm that is the only producer of a good but faces competition from imports that are imperfect substitutes for its products. The firm will always have some monopoly power; even under free trade it will face a downward-sloping demand curve. We denote by $p(X, p_1)$ its demand function, where X represents output and p_1 represents the domestic consumer price of imports, that is, inclusive of tariffs or quota rents.

A tariff (here again the tariff can be specific or ad valorem) will have one definite effect: by raising the price of competing imports from $p_1 = p_1^*$ to $p_1 = p_1^* + t$, it will increase the demand for the domestic firm's output at any given price p. However, the domestic firm might take advantage of this increase in demand by holding its price constant and allowing its sales to rise; in this case we would not register any increase in monopoly power as measured by the ratio of price to marginal costs (or marginal revenue), as long as marginal costs are constant. Or, it may raise both sales and price; then we would register an increase in monopoly power. Which case applies depends on the shift of the marginal revenue curve. Be it as it may, the comparison with a quota does not require this information. It is definite that a quota creates more monopoly power than a tariff.

To see this, we need to think about how a quota works in the imperfect substitutes case. The higher the price of the domestic good, the greater will be the demand for the imports that substitute for this good. However, if these imports are limited by a binding quota, their supply cannot increase. Instead, their price must increase: the quota rents must rise to clear the import market. This means that when the domestic firm is protected by an import quota, it knows that when it raises its price, the prices of imports to domestic consumers will increase as well—a fact that it will take into account in calculating its demand curve.

Figure 3.7 shows what this implies for the comparison of tariffs and quotas. The curve D_t represents the demand facing the domestic

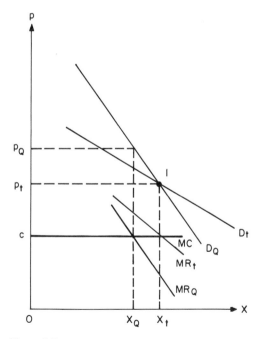

Figure 3.7

firm when protected by some particular tariff rate. MR_t is the corresponding marginal revenue curve, and hence X_t is the profit-maximizing output and p_t the resulting price. Now suppose that the tariff were replaced by a quota limiting imports to their level under the tariff. If the price charged by the domestic firm were unchanged, the quota rent would equal the previous tariff, and there would be no change in the demand for domestic output. Thus the demand curve D_Q corresponding to the quota passes through the original price/ production point 1. However, the new demand curve is *steeper*. The reason is that a rise in the price of the domestic good will pull the price of competing imports to consumers up with it, dampening the negative effect on sales.[3] Because the demand curve with a quota is steeper, the corresponding marginal revenue curve MR_Q lies below MR_t. The result is that the output under quota protection X_Q is lower, and the price p_Q higher, than under the tariff that yields the same level of imports. The imperfect-substitutes case, then, appears to confirm broadly the results of the perfect substitutes case.

3.2 Noncooperative Domestic Oligopoly

The case of a single domestic firm whose only competition comes from imports is, as we have just seen, one whose simplicity allows us to derive strong results with a minimum of technical difficulty. However, as a guide to real-world policy the monopoly analysis presents problems, since what one typically finds in practice is a domestic oligopoly: a small number of firms, but not one, that receive protection in the form of tariffs and quotas. The question is therefore whether insights from studying the monopoly case hold up when there are several domestic firms.

There is unfortunately no general theory of oligopoly behavior. We therefore need to make some additional assumptions about how firms behave in order to complete our model. In our first pass we assume that firms behave *noncooperatively*, that is, that they take one another's actions as given. We discuss tacit collusion in the next section.

---

3. Formally, the domestic demand for imports is given by the inverse demand function $p_1(Q, p)$. The price of domestic output under the tariff equals $p(X, p_1 + t)$ and is implicitly defined by $p = p [X, p_1 (Q, p)]$ under the quota. Hence the slope of the tariff constrained demand curve equals p_1, and the slope of the quota constrained demand curve equals $p_1/(1 - p_2p_{12})$. The latter is larger (in absolute value) under the reasonable assumption $p_2p_{12} < 1$.

Once we have decided to model the behavior of firms as being noncooperative, there remains the question of what it is that firms take as given—the issue of *strategic variable*. Does a firm assume that its competitors will choose a price and adjust output to meet demand at that price, or that they will choose levels of output and adjust their prices so as to be able to sell all their output, or that they set some more complex trade-off between price and output? The two simple extremes of price-setting and quantity-setting are the famous cases of Bertrand and Cournot competition. As it turns out, the qualitative results are pretty much the same. The analysis in the Cournot case is somewhat simpler, however, and so we focus on that case.

We suppose that there are n domestic firms producing the same good that is, however, an imperfect substitute for an imported good. As before, the demand function for the domestic good may be written as $p(X, p_1)$. We assume that the n domestic firms all have the same, constant marginal cost c; this implies that any equilibrium will be *symmetric*—that is, each domestic firm will produce a quantity $x = X/n$. This assumption of symmetry is a very useful simplification, allowing us to draw a direct parallel between equilibrium under oligopoly and monopoly.

Free trade equilibrium is illustrated in figure 3.8, which looks a great deal like figure 3.7. There is a downward-sloping demand curve corresponding to an import price equal to the world price p_1^*, and equilibrium is at point 1, where marginal revenue equals marginal cost.

However, the marginal revenue that is equated to marginal cost is *not* the marginal revenue that corresponds to the demand curve. Instead, it is the marginal revenue *perceived* by firms, defined by

$$\widetilde{MR}(X, p_1) = p(X, p_1) + \left(\frac{X}{n}\right) p_1(X, p_1).$$

It results from the fact that every firm calculates its marginal revenue, taking as given not only the price of foreign imports but also the output level of its domestic rivals. Namely, its marginal revenue equals the change in $xp(X^- + x, p_1)$ when x changes by one unit and X^-—the output of domestic rivals—does not change. In a symmetrical equilibrium $x = X/n$, and perceived marginal revenue is as described above.

This perceived marginal revenue curve is a weighted average of the true marginal revenue curve and the demand curve:

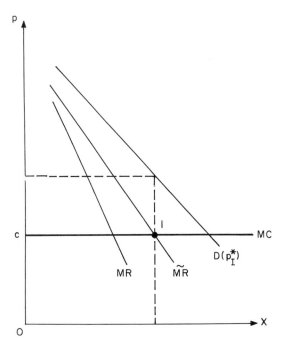

Figure 3.8

$$\widetilde{MR}(X, p_I) = \left(\frac{1}{n}\right) MR(X, p_I) + \left(1 - \frac{1}{n}\right) p(X\, p_I),$$

where $MR(X, p_I) = p(X, p_I) + Xp_I(X, p_I)$. Equilibrium obtains where perceived marginal revenue crosses marginal cost, at point 1.

Effects of a Quota

Now suppose that a tariff is replaced with an import quota that limits imports to the same level. Then just as in the case of a single domestic firm, each of the competing domestic firms will now believe that when it restricts its output, the attempts of consumers to shift their demand to imports will be frustrated by a rise in the quota rent. Each firm still takes the output of other firms as given, so that the demand curve it perceives still takes into account the loss of sales to other firms, but the elimination of the substitution into imports makes this perceived demand curve steeper than before. Thus perceived marginal revenue falls, and firms are induced to reduce their output and increase their prices. A quota, then, creates more monopoly power for the domestic industry than an equivalent tariff.

Our examination of the noncooperative oligopoly case seems clearly to confirm the intuitions from the monopoly case. Tariffs increase monopoly power, quotas increase them even more. Our next step is to consider the more difficult question of what happens when the domestic industry may act collusively rather than noncooperatively.

3.3 Collusive Domestic Oligopoly

If firms were to collude perfectly, the study of oligopoly would be no different from that of monopoly. What gives collusion its interest and also its difficulty is the likelihood that firms cannot monitor and enforce agreements perfectly, and that the extent to which they can exploit their potential joint monopoly power depends on the environment—including the trade policy environment. In reality the ability of firms to collude no doubt depends on a variety of factors, including antitrust law, information issues, and even the social cohesion of the industry's executives. In recent work in industrial organization, however, interesting insights have been gained through an approach that strips the problem of collusion down to only one issue: whether the expected costs resulting from a breakdown of a cartel or tacit collusion are sufficient to deter cheating. We assume that even in cases of explicit collusion the agreements have to be self-enforcing; otherwise, we have a monopolylike situation.

The basic idea is that at any point in time a firm can always increase its profits by breaking cartel discipline and undercutting its rivals' price. However, if it does so, the cartel is likely to collapse, reducing the subsequent profits of all participants. If the cartel is going to be sustainable, the costs to each member firm of its collapse must outweigh the gains from cheating. Under some circumstances the need for sustainability will constrain the ability of the cartel to raise prices above their noncooperative level; if too high a price makes cheating attractive, the cartel must keep the price just below the level that provides a critical level of temptation (see Tirole 1988, ch. 6).

When this idea is applied to trade policy, as was done by Rotemberg and Saloner (1988), a seemingly paradoxical result emerges: a quota may raise prices less than a tariff, precisely because it raises profits in the absence of a cartel. If profits will be higher in the absence of a cartel than they would be otherwise, the costs of cheating and bringing the cartel down will be smaller, and hence the cartel must make cheating less attractive by lowering its target price.

We consider an underlying industry structure identical to that we considered in the last section. There are several domestic firms producing a good that is an imperfect substitute for an imported good that is supplied competitively at a fixed price. When the firms are behaving noncooperatively, they play Cournot: each takes the output of the others as given, although they do recognize that when an import quota is in place they can affect the consumer price of the imported good.

The model is extended in two ways. First, the firms are now assumed to be in a competition that extends indefinitely into the future; they care not only about current profits but about profits in future periods, discounted at some rate r. Second, the firms can form a cartel, that is, they can discuss and agree on a price that they will jointly charge. The fly in the ointment is that there is no direct enforcement mechanism compelling firms to honor their agreements. The cartel will therefore work only if the agreement the firms reach is self-enforcing.

Finally, we need a rule for what happens if a firm fails to honor its agreement. Many scenarios are possible, but here we focus on the simplest: if a firm defects, everyone else remains at the cartel output for one period, then plays noncooperatively forever after. Note that this implies that a "period" is effectively the length of time it takes before other firms notice and react to a firm's decision to defect.

In models of tacit collusion there exist many equilibria. In what follows we focus on the most collusive choice; the outcome that maximizes profits. We may indeed expect to observe this outcome whenever there exists an explicit agreement, even if an outside party, such as a court, has no authority to enforce it.

Determination of the Cartel Price and Output

Whatever the trade regime, a firm has two options: cooperate with the cartel or defect. The period after it defects, the cartel collapses, and what is left is a noncooperative outcome. Let x be the output per firm agreed on by the cartel; then the firm's decision depends on the comparison of three values. $\pi_C(x)$ denotes the firm's per-period profits under the cartel; $\pi_D(x)$ denotes its profits if it defects and all other firms produce x; and π_N are its per-period profits in the absence of (or following the collapse of) a cartel (the noncooperative profit level).

If it stays with the cartel, the cartel will go on indefinitely, and the firm's present value will equal the capitalized value of the profit stream; that is, $\pi_C(x)/r$. If the firm defects, it will earn higher profits in the first period, $\pi_D(x)$, but lower thereafter, π_N. The present value of profits of a defecting firm equals $\pi_D(x) + \pi_N/(1 + r)r$.

Now when firms set a cartel price and quantity, they will be aware that each of them will subsequently face this choice. There will be no point in setting up a cartel from which everyone immediately defects, so the effort will be to maximize profits subject to the constrain that nobody has an incentive to cheat. That is, the cartel's objective will be

Max $\pi_C(x)$
$\quad x$

such that

$$\frac{\pi_C(x)}{r} \geq \pi_D(x) + \frac{\pi_N}{(1 + r)r} \; .$$

Under some circumstances the constraint will force the cartel to produce a larger output than the profit-maximizing output x_M.

Figure 3.9 shows the situation in which the constraint does bind

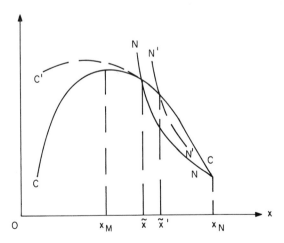

Figure 3.9

the cartel. The figure shows how the present values of the "cooperate" and "defect" strategies depend on the cartel output (and therefore price). If firms cooperate, their present values look like the solid curve CC: rising at first as output per firm is reduced below the noncooperative output x_N and reaching a maximum at the joint profit-maximizing output x_M. If an individual firm cheats, its present value will follow the solid curve NN. This curve is always downward-sloping, since the firm is always at least as profitable when rival firms produce less. If it is as drawn in figure 3.9, cutting CC from above to the right of x_M, then the cartel is constrained: it cannot set an output below $\tilde{x}$ without providing an incentive to defect. Thus in this case the cartel output per firm will be set precisely at $\tilde{x}$.

There are two other possibilities, illustrated in figures 3.10 and 3.11. In figure 3.10 the curve NN cuts CC to the left of x_M; in this case the enforceability constraint is not binding, and the cartel behaves like a profit-maximizing monopolist. In figure 3.11 NN lies above CC for all outputs below x_N. In this case *any* attempt to raise the price above its noncooperative level will lead to cheating, so no cartel is possible.

There is of course no reason why NN cannot cross CC several times. In this case, however, the cartel will simply set output at the lowest point where NN cuts CC from above. So this case is in its implication exactly the same as the others.

Clearly, the special features of collusive oligopoly, as opposed to

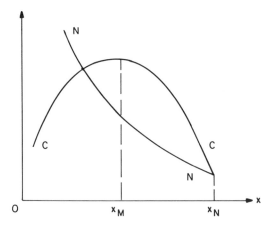

Figure 3.10

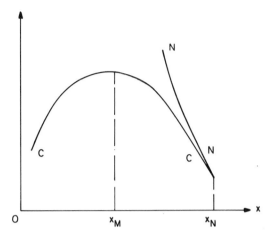

Figure 3.11

noncooperative oligopoly or monopoly, occur only when a cartel is possible, but its actions are limited by problems of enforceability. We therefore now focus on the case illustrated in figure 3.9, where enforceability limits the cartel price.

Comparing Tariffs and Quotas

When enforceability constrains cartel pricing, the effects of trade policy may be very different from their effects under either monopoly or noncooperative oligopoly. In particular, we can establish a definite, surprising result: a quota that limits imports not to exceed their free trade level *lowers* the price that the cartel is able to charge (see Rotemberg and Saloner 1988).

Suppose that the solid curves *NN* and *CC* in figure 3.9 correspond to the situation under free trade. When we limit imports not to exceed their free trade level, the curves shift in directions illustrated by the broken lines.

First, consider *CC*, defined as $\pi_C(x)/r$. This is just a monopolist's profit function (blown up by the division by r). What a quota does is give the monopolist a demand curve that passes through the original price/production point, so at an unchanged output profits do not change: $C'C'$ passes through CC at the original cartel price and quantity. However, as we know from our discussion in previous sections, at prices above the original one the new demand curve is steeper, so that profits are higher at lower outputs. Thus $C'C'$ lies above CC at points to the left of $\bar{x}$. It coincides with CC to the right of $\bar{x}$.

NN is the sum of two components: the profitability of defecting and the present value of the noncooperative profits that follow as a consequence. We focus on what happens at the original output $\bar{x}$. At this price, if one firm cheats, it will cut into imports as well as other domestic sales, so the quota will not be binding; thus $\pi_D(\bar{x})$ is unchanged. However, the profitability of firms in the noncooperative equilibrium may be increased. Thus at the original price the penalty for cheating may be reduced, implying that at least in the neighborhood of $\bar{x}$ the curve NN shifts up.[4]

The result is now apparent: the minimum output that the cartel can produce without inducing defection rises from $\bar{x}$ to $\bar{x}'$. An import quota actually leads to a rise in the domestic industry's output (and consequently a fall in the domestic price). By reducing the penalty to cheating, the quota forces the cartel to set prices lower and thus reduce the temptation.

An important additional observation in this case is that the import quota that accomplishes this will not actually be binding. To see this, note that we have set the quota equal to the original free trade level of imports. However, the cartel responds by cutting its price, reducing import demand below its free trade level, so that the actual level of imports is less than the quota limit. This is another example of the principle we found in the case of the import competing monopolist: policies that affect the *threat* of import competition can alter incentives even when they leave the actual level of imports unchanged.

References

Bhagwati, Jagdish, N. (1965). "On the equivalence of tariffs and quotas." In Robert E. Baldwin et al. (eds.), *Trade, Growth and the Balance of Payments: Essays in Honor of Gottfried Haberler*. Chicago: Rand McNally.

---

4. We say *may* be reduced because the output of domestic firms is larger under the noncooperative outcome than under the cartel, so the level of imports in the noncooperative solution will be less. But this means that a quota at the cartel level may not be binding in the noncooperative case, in which case it has no effect. However, as we know from previous analysis, a quota that exceeds the free trade level of imports may still raise prices and profits, as long as it does not exceed that level by too much.

Corden, Max W. (1974). *Trade Policy and Economic Welfare*. Oxford: Clarendon Press.

Rotemberg, Julio J., and Saloner, Garth (1988). "Tariffs vs. quotas with implicit collusion." *Canadian Journal of Economics*, forthcoming.

Tirole, Jean (1988). *The Theory of Industrial Organization*. Cambridge, MA: MIT Press.

In the preceding chapter we considered the effects of trade policies that protect an imperfectly competitive domestic industry from competitive foreign suppliers. In this chapter we turn to the converse situation: trade policy applied to imperfectly competitive foreign exporters who face either no domestic competitors or a perfectly competitive domestic industry.

Although the situation considered here is symmetric to that considered in chapter 3, the difference in the characteristics of the problem means a substantial difference in focus. Except for some very special cases, protecting an imperfectly competitive domestic industry reduces national welfare; thus the analysis in chapter 3 was necessarily a positive analysis of what happens if a government happens to pursue such a policy, rather than a normative analysis of what a government should do. The best we could do by way of prescriptions was to describe "second-worst" policies: for a given degree of import restriction, a tariff was not as bad as a quota. By contrast, when trade policies are applied against foreign firms with market power there is, as we will see, a real possibility that the importing country may gain—in effect, that it can use trade policy to recapture some of the monopoly rents these foreign firms are extracting from domestic consumers. This means that in this chapter we will also want to explore this justification, and ask both what the first-best policies for such rent extraction are and whether other policies can be justified with second-best arguments. At the same time, however, we want to engage in positive analysis as well, asking how standard policies such as tariffs and quotas affect trade when the exporting firms are imperfectly competitive.

As in chapter 3 we build from the simple to the more complex: starting with the basic case of a foreign monopolist, we move on first to foreign oligopoly and then to a foreign cartel. In the first seven sections we do not discuss ad valorem tariffs or import subsidies. The important difference between these instruments when foreigners have market power is explained in section 4.8.

4.1 Optimal Policies against a Foreign Monopolist

Consider a foreign firm that is the single foreign supplier of a commodity to the domestic market. We assume either that there is no domestic supply or that the domestic industry is perfectly competitive, so that domestic demand for imports can simply be expressed as a downward-sloping demand curve whose elasticity determines the foreign firm's monopoly power.

Figure 4.1 shows the foreign firm's choice of exports for the case in which marginal costs of supplying the domestic market are constant at the level c^*. The domestic demand curve for imports is D and the associated marginal revenue curve is MR.[1] Profit maximizing exports are m_M, determined by the intersection of the marginal cost and the marginal revenue curves. The firm charges p_M^*. The welfare gain from these imports to the importing country is measured by the

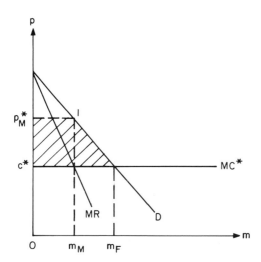

Figure 4.1

---

1. Here we assume that the demand curve is smooth; that is, there are no kinks. The possibility of a kink is discussed at a later stage.

area above the horizontal line passing through point 1 and below the demand curve.

The government of the importing country would like to increase domestic welfare. In this simple case it can do this in a surprisingly simple way: by imposing a maximum price on the foreign supplier. As is familiar from price control analysis in a domestic context, a monopolist's price can be restricted to some degree without leading to excess demand, because his price is initially above marginal costs; this means that even a price somewhat below its *laissez-faire* level still provides the firm with an adequate incentive to produce as much as consumers want to purchase. On the other hand, the foreign monopolist will not export for a price below marginal cost c^*. Therefore, when the sole concern is the private sector's welfare level, the first-best policy is to impose a price ceiling on imports at the level c^*. This guarantees the lowest unit cost of imports and a domestic price that equals marginal costs of imports, ensuring the highest welfare level. The resulting welfare gain is described by the shaded area. The optimal price ceiling brings about a price reduction from p_M^* to c^* and an import rise from m_M to m_F.

The adequacy of a price ceiling by itself to extract all foreign rents depends on the assumption that foreign marginal costs are flat. This is a kind of small-country assumption. If it is not satisfied, then a full extraction of rents from the foreign firm is more difficult. To extract all rent, the domestic government would have to be able to bargain with the foreign firm, charging it a flat fee for the right to sell in the domestic market as well as limiting its price.

The case in which the foreign monopolist's marginal costs are rising with exports is illustrated in figure 4.2. Without policy intervention, imports are m_M and domestic and import prices are p_M^*. If the domestic government could bargain with the foreign monopolist and extract its entire producer surplus (profits or rewards to fixed factors of production), its best bargain would be to import m_F units at variable costs to the monopolist, the latter being represented by the area below the MC^* curve up to m_F. Optimality of this outcome is seen by observing that it provides the importing country with the surplus represented by the area above the horizontal line passing through point 1 and below the demand curve, plus the additional surplus represented by the area below this line and above the MC^* curve. This is achieved by selling imports in the domestic market at price p (on the horizontal line through point 1)—which provides the first

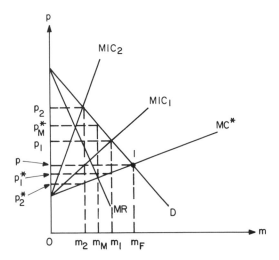

Figure 4.2

component of the surplus—and cashing in in the form of government revenue the difference between revenue accruing from these sales and the actual import costs (the second component). The latter can be redistributed back to the public in a lump-sum fashion. Since goods cannot be obtained at lower cost than their costs to the monopolist, this represents the largest sum of consumer surplus, producer surplus, and revenue that can possibly be appropriated.

The idea that the government can drive so hard and precise a bargain seems fairly unrealistic, however. So it is interesting to ask what can be achieved with a price ceiling in the absence of any fee for the right to sell in the domestic market. To determine an optimal price ceiling of this type, observe first that the price ceiling can always be used to force the foreign firm to behave like a competitive industry. In particular, a price ceiling of $p_c = p$ will lead the monopolist to provide the same levels of imports, at the same price, as a competitive foreign industry would have provided under free trade. However, as we know from chapter 2, when foreign marginal cost is upward sloping, the marginal cost of imports to a country exceeds the import price, and optimal policy even for competitive suppliers—or for a foreign monopolist forced to behave like a competitive industry—involves driving a wedge between the landed price of imports and the price paid by domestic consumers. Thus in figure 4.2 the country's total import costs are $mMC^*(m)$, where m represents imports.

The optimal policy involves maximization of consumer surplus, plus domestic producer surplus and government revenue. This is achieved by setting the domestic price equal to marginal import costs $MC^* + m\,dMC^*/dm$. If MIC_1 in figure 4.2 represents the marginal import cost curve, then the optimal policy is to set the import price ceiling at p_1^* and the domestic price at p_1, collecting the difference either with a tariff or with auctioned-off quota licenses. This results in a government revenue of $(p_1 - p_1^*)m_1$.

In the figure as we have drawn it the domestic price p_1 is lower than the monopoly price p_M^* and imports are higher than m_M. This need not, however, be the case. If MIC_2 happens to be the marginal cost of imports curve, then the resulting domestic price p_2 is higher than the monopoly price and imports m_2 are lower than m_M. Both cases are possible. The former, in which the optimal price ceiling leads to an expansion of imports and a decline in domestic price, occurs when the monopolist's marginal costs rise slowly with exports relative to the decline of marginal revenue. The latter occurs when the opposite is true. An interesting implication is that optimal policy can be more restrictive in terms of imports than free trade.

4.2 Trade Taxes

Price ceilings on imports are not a commonly observed policy. On the other hand, trade taxes are often used in order to achieve advantages in foreign trade. It is therefore natural to ask whether the arguments that we showed lead to a recommendation of price ceilings as first-best policies can be used to justify tariffs as a second-best policy. To separate this issue from the optimal tariff argument in the competitive case, we assume that the foreign monopolist's marginal costs are constant.

We can immediately show that it is at least possible that tariffs can raise national welfare when applied against a foreign monopolist. Figure 4.3 shows the case of a linear demand function. In the absence of intervention the monopolist sets price p_M and exports m_M.

Now suppose that a specific tariff of size t is imposed. The tariff raises the monopolist's marginal export costs to $c^* + t$, at which he chooses to charge price p_t and export m_t. Consequently consumer plus producer surplus declines by the area trapped between points 12345. This represents a loss to the economy. On the othe hand, the government collects tariff revenue tm_t, which is represented by the

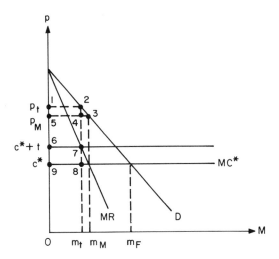

Figure 4.3

area between points 6789. The net welfare effect is the difference between lost surplus and tariff revenue. When the demand curve is linear, however, its slope equals half the slope of the marginal revenue curve. Therefore the area between points 1245 equals half the area between points 6789. The implication is that revenue exceeds lost consumer surplus if the triangle 234 is sufficiently small. However, this triangle is proportional to the *square* of the tariff rate so that it must be outweighed by the gains for a sufficiently small tariff. Thus we conclude that small tariffs are desirable (see Brander and Spencer 1984a for the original argument).

Does this result generalize beyond linear demand curves? Whatever the demand curve, we can measure the loss in consumer surplus by an area such as 12345 and tariff revenue by an area such as 6789. In addition in each case a triangle such as 234 is second order, that is, can be ignored if we consider sufficiently small tariffs. So for the question of whether any tariff is justifiable we need only ask whether the revenue 6789 exeeds 1245. This will be true if and only if the demand curve is flatter than the marginal revenue curve at m_M. Hence this relative slope determines whether a small tariff is welfare improving. In the linear demand case a small tariff raises welfare precisely because with linear demand the marginal revenue curve is steeper than the demand curve. This, however, is not always the case. Figure 4.4 shows the case of a constant elasticity demand func-

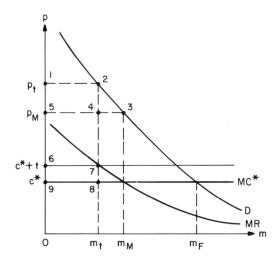

Figure 4.4

tion, for which the slope of the marginal revenue curve is $1 - \epsilon$ times the slope of the demand curve, where $1 > \epsilon > 0$ denotes the elasticity of demand. Clearly, in this case a tariff is harmful. By implication, a small import *subsidy* benefits the country (see the diagram in figure 4.5 which represents a subsidy of size s). We conclude that tariffs should be used as a second-best policy when marginal revenue declines faster than price and that import subsidies should be used when marginal revenue declines slower than price. Welfare-improving trade taxes lead to a contraction of imports in the former case and to an expansion in the latter.

We have analyzed the possibility of welfare-improving tariffs in terms of the effects on revenue and consumer surplus; however, it is equally valid to think of them in terms of their effects on the importing country's terms of trade. An increase in the specific tariff by one unit reduces the monopolist's exports by a quantity that equals the slope of the marginal revenue curve relative to the vertical axis; that is, by $-1/MR'$. On the other hand, an import contraction of one unit increases domestic price by the slope of the demand curve; that is, by $-p'$. Therefore a unit tariff increase increases domestic price by p'/MR'. Since the import price equals $p - t$, the unit tariff increase reduces the import price and improves the terms of trade if and only if p'/MR' is smaller than one (if and only if the marginal revenue curve is steeper than the demand curve). This point

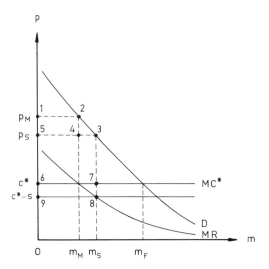

Figure 4.5

is evident from our figures. It also emerges from the general formula for welfare change (2.4).

4.3 Quotas

We have shown that a tariff improves welfare in some circumstances and an import subsidy in others. This raises two related questions. First, is a quota ever desirable? And second, how does it differ from a tariff? We assume for the most part that quotas are administered by licensing domestic residents to import. Only at the end of the chapter do we take up voluntary export restraints.

First, we note that an import quota cannot help when the optimal tariff is negative, namely, when marginal revenue is flatter than demand. Because in this case it is desirable to expand rather than to contract imports. In particular, if we set the import quota at the level of imports induced by an import subsidy, it will not be binding; the quota exceeds m_M, and the foreign monopolist chooses to export m_M. To attain the subsidy induced import level, it is necessary to impose a *minimum import requirement* (MIR). When this is done, however, the importing country's welfare is higher under the quantitative restriction than under the import subsidy, because domestic price and quantity are the same in both cases but subsidy costs are saved in the former. This point we demonstrate in figure 4.5. With an import subsidy s, area 12345 represents the gain in surplus while 6789 represents the (smaller) subsidy bill. Imports are m_S and domestic price is p_S. If an MIR of size m_S is used instead, imports and consumer price are the same. Therefore the gain in surplus is the same, but we save the subsidy bill under the MIR.

The subsidy constitutes a transfer of resources from the importing country to the foreign monopolist, which can be saved by an MIR. Another way to view this gain is as a terms of trade gain. Since (1) in both cases the domestic price is the same, (2) the import price equals the domestic price under the MIR, and (3) the import price equals the domestic price plus the subsidy under the import subsidy policy, the import price is lower under the MIR.

It follows that if MIRs were feasible, they could be used to reach the outcome of an optimal price ceiling. If the MIR were set at m_F, the foreign monopolist would find it profit maximizing to export the minimally required quantity and set its price equal to marginal costs c^*.[2] Hence under these circumstances an MIR is the preferred policy. In fact, it also dominates a tariff when marginal revenue declines faster than price because it attains the allocation of the optimal price ceiling policy, and the latter achieves the first-best outcome.

MIRs aside, an import quota cannot replicate the outcome of an import subsidy when marginal revenue declines slower than price (a case in which an import subsidy raises welfare). In the alternative case—when marginal revenue declines faster than price—a tariff raises welfare and the tariff-restricted imported volume can be attained by means of a quota. Thus, for example, in figure 4.3 the tariff reduces imports to m_t. If a quota of size m_t is installed instead, the foreign monopolist finds it profit maximizing to export the quota constrained quantity. Hence in both cases imports, consumption, and domestic price are the same. Nevertheless, the two policies have different welfare implications; *the tariff dominates the quota because under the quota the equivalent of tariff revenue accrues to the foreign monopolist.*

This fact is evident from an analysis of the monopolist's decision

---

2. This is necessarily the case when marginal revenue is nonnegative at m_F. If, however, marginal revenue is negative at this quantity, a monopolist who is forced to export the required minimum chooses to destroy part of it after meeting the import requirement (provided destruction costs are nil). In this case consumption is lower than m_F, and the consumer price is higher than c^*. The discussion in the text excludes this possibility.

under a quota. With the quota in place the demand curve that he faces consists of the original demand curve for quantities below m_t, and it becomes vertical at the quota limit m_t. Since p_t exceeds his marginal costs, the profit-maximizing strategy is to export up to the quota limit and sell at price p_t. It is therefore clear that in this case a tariff dominates a quota because it increases the importing country's income by tm_t (see Shibata 1968 for the original argument), or alternatively, the tariff generates better terms of trade. Moreover, *in contrast to a small tariff, a quota reduces welfare* because it reduces consumer surplus without generating revenue to the government or profits to domestic importers; the quota rent is appropriated by the foreign monopolist. We conclude that in the presence of a foreign monopolist a tariff dominates a quota and a quota is, in fact, harmful (see Krishna 1988a for some extensions).

4.4* Optimal Trade Taxes

So far we have focused on determining the *sign* of desirable trade policies. In particular, we have identified circumstances in which tariffs or import subsidies are desirable. We did, however, leave open the question of the optimal level of these instruments.

One general point can be made at the outset: when a tariff is beneficial, it pays to raise it as long as the marginal loss of consumer plus producer surplus falls short of the marginal gain from tariff revenue, and when an import subsidy is beneficial it pays to raise it as long as the marginal gain of consumer plus producer surplus exceeds the marginal subsidy bill. An instrument reaches its optimal level when the marginal loss (gain) of surplus just equals the marginal gain (loss) in revenue.

To derive the optimal tax, we use formula (2.6) for welfare changes, which reduces in the current context to

$$dU = -(dp - dt)m + tdm.$$

Denoting by $p(m)$ the inverse import demand function and by $m(t)$ and $U(t)$ imports and welfare as functions of the tariff level, we obtain

$$U'(t) = - \{p'[m(t)]m'(t) - 1\}m(t) + tm'(t). \tag{4.1}$$

This equation corresponds to the standard representation of welfare gains from trade taxes; the first expression represents the terms of trade effect while the second represents the tax-wedge effect. The tax-wedge effect equals the initial divergence between the domestic and import price times the change in imports. The terms of trade effect can be recognized as follows: The import price equals $p[m(t)]$ − t. Therefore the increase in the import price as a result of a tax increase equals $p'm' - 1$. The welfare loss from a terms of trade deterioration equals the increase in the import price times the import volume (see also Jones 1987 on this point).

It is clear from this representation that a small tariff benefits the importing country if and only if $U'(0) > 0$, which requires a terms of trade improvement. In a competitive setup a small tariff has either no effect or improves the terms of trade. What we have shown is that in the presence of a foreign monopolist a small tariff improves the terms of trade only if marginal revenue declines faster than price. If it does not, an import subsidy improves the terms of trade.

The optimal tax is attained when $U'(t) = 0$. Therefore the optimal tax is implicitly defined by

$$t = m(t) \left\{ p' \left[m(t)\right] - \frac{1}{m'(t)} \right\} . \tag{4.2}$$

This formula does not depend on market structure in the foreign country; it applies to the case of a foreign monopolist as well as to other cases, such as a foreign oligopoly. Foreign market structure affects the shape of $m(t)$, thereby affecting the optimal tax *level* but not the tax *formula*. A negative tax represents a subsidy.

A foreign monopolist chooses exports so as to equate marginal revenue to marginal costs. In this case we represent $m(t)$ in implicit form by

$$MR[m(t)] = c^* + t,$$

where $MR(m) \equiv p(m) + mp'(m)$. This implies that $m'(t) = 1/MR'[m(t)]$. Upon substitution into (4.2) we obtain the optimal tax formula for the monopoly case (see Brander and Spencer 1984a):

$$t = m(t) \left\{ p'[m(t)] - MR'[m(t)] \right\} . \tag{4.3}$$

Clearly, the optimal tax is positive—namely, a tariff—whenever the slope of the marginal revenue curve $(-MR')$ exceeds the slope of the demand curve $(-p')$, and it is negative—namely, a subsidy—whenever the marginal revenue curve is flatter than the demand curve.

4.5 Kinked Demand

So far our analysis has relied on the assumption that the import demand function is smooth. In the presence of competing domestic supply, however, it is likely that this will not be the case. We reexamine our conclusions in view of this possibility. In figure 4.6, Panel (a) presents domestic demand and supply curves. Domestic output is positive for prices larger than $\underline{p}$. We depict the derived demand curve for imports in panel (b); it has a kink at price $\underline{p}$. The kink introduces a discontinuity in the import marginal revenue curve; marginal revenue drops from point 1 to 2 as imports change from $\underline{m}^-$ to $\underline{m}^+$. If the relevant import range is below $\underline{m}$ or above it, then the previous conclusions remain valid. If, however, this is not the case, new possibilities arise.

Consider, for example, a case in which the foreign monopolist's marginal cost curve passes between points 1 and 2, as drawn in the figure. In this case the monopoly price equals $\underline{p}$, namely, the highest price that prevents domestic production of import competing goods. Now every tariff in the range zero to $t_1 = p_1 - c^*$ raises revenue without altering imports or price. Hence tariffs within this range bring about a nondistorting transfer from the foreign monopolist to

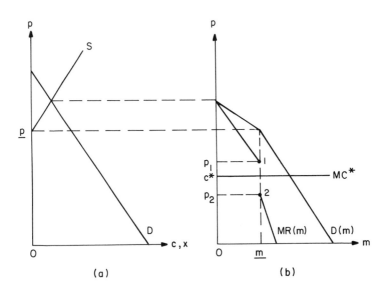

Figure 4.6

the domestic government (see Brander and Spencer 1981). If at import levels smaller than $\underline{m}$ marginal revenue falls faster than price, the importing country benefits from raising the tariff beyond t_1. In fact, in this case the optimal tariff formula (4.3) applies. If, however, marginal revenue declines slower than price (as in the case of a constant elasticity demand function), an import subsidy may not be desirable.

A small import subsidy leads to welfare losses because, so long as it is smaller than $s_2 = c^* - p_2$, no change takes place in imports or domestic price. Hence within this range the subsidy brings about a transfer from the importing country to the foreign monopolist without additional effects. Starting with s_2, further increases in the subsidy lead to net gains. However, so long as these net gains do not exceed the initially unprofitable subsidy bill $s_2\underline{m}$, the overall effect of the subsidy is harmful. It might in fact be the case that the optimal subsidy—which satisfies condition (4.3)—reduces welfare. Moreover even the most beneficial subsidy may not represent the optimal trade policy. When marginal revenue declines slower than price, the subsidy that satisfies (4.3) is the optimal trade policy if and only if it produces net welfare gains that exceed $t_1\underline{m}$. If it does not, the country does better with a tariff of size t_1. This shows that in the presence of a kink in the import demand curve, we need to provide a global comparison of optimal policies and cannot rely on local comparisons. It is, for example, clear that when foreign marginal costs are below point 2 and marginal revenue declines more slowly than price, a local analysis indicates that a subsidy is required. It might, however, still be the case that under these circumstances a tariff equal to $p_1 - c^*$ brings about a larger welfare gain.

4.6 Cournot Oligopoly

We now expand our discussion to cover the case of an oligopolistic market structure in the exporting country. Suppose that the foreign export industry consists of n identical firms who play Cournot; we deal with Bertrand competition at a later stage. How useful are trade taxes in this case?

To analyze the behavior of the oligopoly, we use the technique from the last chapter: we define a *perceived marginal revenue curve* $\widetilde{MR}(m, n)$ and determine equilibrium by the equality of perceived marginal revenue and marginal cost. This perceived marginal revenue curve will not be the same as the "true" marginal revenue curve associated with the demand curve, but except for this, the oligopoly can be treated as if it were a monopolist with marginal revenue $\widetilde{MR}(m, n)$.

In a symmetrical Cournot market each firm produces m/n units of the good; its perceived marginal revenue equals

$$\widetilde{MR}(m, n) = p(m) + \left(\frac{m}{n}\right)p'(m).$$

An important point about this perceived marginal revenue is that it is a weighted average of the demand curve and the "true" marginal revenue curve MR:

$$\widetilde{MR}(m, n) = \left(1 - \frac{1}{n}\right)p(m) + \left(\frac{1}{n}\right)MR(m).$$

Since perceived marginal revenue is a weighted average of the demand curve and the marginal revenue curve, its slope lies in between. If marginal revenue is steeper than demand, so is perceived marginal revenue; if marginal revenue is flatter than demand, so is perceived marginal revenue. But this means that the sign of the appropriate policy is the same with Cournot oligopoly as it would be if there were a foreign monopolist. If MR is steeper than demand, a tariff is indicated; if MR is flatter, an import subsidy.

*Optimal policy

Although the sign of the appropriate policy does not change, its magnitude does. To see this, we need to calculate explicitly how a tariff affects imports and prices. First, we note that in equilibrium perceived marginal revenue equals tariff-inclusive marginal cost:

$$\frac{1}{n}MR(m) + \left(1 - \frac{1}{n}\right)p(m) = c^* + t. \tag{4.4}$$

This provides a solution for m as a function of the tax t and the number of firms n, denoted by $m = \mu(t, n)$; in the monopoly case $n = 1$. Clearly, $m'(t) = \mu_t(t, n)$, and

$$\frac{1}{m'} = \frac{1}{n}MR' + \left(1 - \frac{1}{n}\right)p'. \tag{4.5}$$

By substituting (4.5) into (4.1), we obtain

$$U'(0) = - \frac{p'(m) - MR'(m)}{MR'(m) + (n - 1)p'(m)} m,$$

where m solves (4.4) for $t = 0$. We see from this equation that $U'(0) > 0$ so that a small tariff improves the terms of trade when marginal revenue declines faster than price, while $U'(0) < 0$ so that a small import subsidy improves the terms of trade when marginal revenue declines more slowly than price. Hence the conditions under which a tariff or an import subsidy is desirable are the same under monopoly and oligopoly. The size of the optimal tax, however, depends on the number of firms. Substituting (4.5) into the optimal tax formula (4.2) yields

$$t = \frac{m}{n} [p'(m) - MR'(m)]. \tag{4.6}$$

Equations (4.4) and (4.6) jointly determine the optimal tax and the level of imports for a given number of firms. It remains optimal to impose a tariff when marginal revenue declines faster than price and to impose an import subsidy when marginal revenue declines slower than price. But the optimal tax depends on the number of firms, and it approaches zero as n goes to infinity.

4.7* Bertrand Oligopoly

The main results of the previous section remain valid under Bertrand oligopoly, in the sense that welfare effects of trade policy depend on details of demand: for some demand structures, a tariff improves welfare, whereas for others, an import subsidy improves welfare. Moreover in a formal sense the conditions for various outcomes are the same under suitable interpretations of demand and marginal revenue curves.

We now assume that there are n competing imports that are good but not perfect substitutes for each other. We limit our discussion to symmetrical demand functions that have the following form:

$$p_i = p(m_i, P_i), \qquad i = 1, 2, \ldots, n, \tag{4.7}$$

where P_i denotes a price index of all competing goods other than i, defined by

$$P_i = \Phi(p_1, p_2, \ldots, p_{i-1}, p_{i+1}, \ldots, p_n). \tag{4.8}$$

The function $\Phi(\cdot)$ is symmetrical, increasing, positively linear homogeneous, and normalized to satisfy $\Phi(1, 1, \ldots, 1) = 1$. The demand function declines in quantity and increases in price of competing goods. It also satisfies $0 < p_P(m, P) < 1$ for $P = p(m, P)$; that is, an increase in the price index raises the demand price of a good by less than the price index rise.

Figure 4.7 shows the determination of price and quantity in this market. Exploiting the symmetry between firms, we draw a pari passu demand curve $\tilde{D}$—that is, we show how the price of the representative firm falls when all firms increase their output together. What we do is define a function $\tilde{P}(m)$, implicitly described by $P = p(m, P)$. Clearly, under our assumptions this is a downward-sloping curve.

A typical foreign exporter chooses his price to maximize profits, taking as given the pricing policy of his competitors. This involves setting marginal cost equal to *perceived marginal revenue* $\widetilde{MR}(m)$:

$$\widetilde{MR}(m) = \tilde{P}(m) + p_m[m, \tilde{P}(m)]m = c^* + t.$$

Point 1 identifies equilibrium imports m_t. The corresponding price p_t is found on the demand curve.

It should now be apparent that the effect of a tariff in this case is

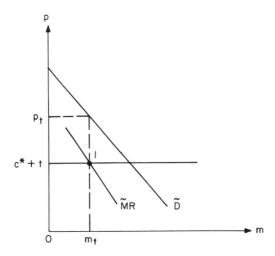

Figure 4.7

completely analogous to its effect on a monopolist. A one-unit increase in the tariff will push the representative foreign firm back along the $\widetilde{MR}$ curve, with $dm = 1/\widetilde{MR}'$; this will raise the price paid by domestic consumers by $dp = \bar{P}'dm = \bar{P}'/\widetilde{MR}'$. Thus the price received by the representative foreign firm will rise or fall depending on whether $\bar{P}'$ is greater or less than $\widetilde{MR}'$—that is, on whether the pari passu demand curve is steeper or flatter than the perceived marginal revenue curve. If the perceived marginal revenue curve is steeper, a tariff will improve the importing country's terms of trade, and thus a positive tariff will be optimal. It is now straighforward to derive the optimal trade tax, using the procedure described for the Cournot case. The resulting formula is also analogous to the Cournot case.

Although we find a close analogy in results between Bertrand and Cournot conduct, we need to be cautious in their interpretation. The point is, of course, that the perceived marginal revenue curves are not constructed in the same way and the relevant demand functions are also different. The spirit of the results is, however, the same.

4.8 Ad Valorem Trade Taxes

In this chapter our discussion of trade taxes has so far been restricted to specific tariffs and subsidies, where the tax or subsidy is a fixed sum per physical unit. In real life it is more common for taxes and subsidies to be specified in ad valorem terms, that is, as a percentage of the selling price. In a perfectly competitive industry this makes no difference: as long as a specific and an ad valorem tax drive the same wedge between producer and consumer prices, they have the same effect. In the current context, however, there is a difference.

To see why, consider the following simple example. Suppose that a foreign monopolist sells into our market and that we have imposed the optimal specific tariff against him. This tariff, we assume, is at the rate of one dollar per unit, and the monopolist's selling price ex tax is ten dollars per unit. Now suppose that we replace the specific tax with an ad valorem tariff of 10 percent. If the monopolist were to leave his price unchanged at ten dollars, the tax per unit would still be one dollar, and nothing would change. But he will not: the change in the form of the tax will lead him to lower his price.

The reason is that the demand curve faced by the monopolist now becomes flatter. With the specific tariff, if the monopolist were to cut his price by one dollar, the price to consumers would also fall by one dollar. With a 10 percent ad valorem tariff, cutting his price by one dollar will reduce the prices to consumers by $1.10, and therefore generate a larger increase in sales. Thus a price reduction that would not have been profitable with a specific tariff will be profitable under an ad valorem tariff.

Clearly, then, there is always an ad valorem tariff that yields better results for the importing country than the optimal specific tariff (since the tariff that would have been equivalent to the optimal specific tariff at the original prices is definitely better, and there may be a tax rate that is better still).

What about subsidies? Here the result is reversed. Suppose that the optimal ad valorem subsidy to a foreign monopolist that charges ten dollars is 10 percent. Then the foreign firm knows that if it cuts its price by one dollar, the consumer price falls by only 90 cents. If a subsidy of one dollar per unit is used instead, then any price reduction will be fully passed on to consumers. So there is always a specific subsidy that is better than the optimal ad valorem subsidy.

Two additional implications of this comparison should be noted. First, if only ad valorem tariffs and subsidies are available, tariffs look better and subsidies worse than our analysis has suggested so far. That is, there is an additional presumption in favor of import tariffs when ad valorem instruments are used.

Second, we note that even the sign of the optimal policy may depend on the kind of instrument available. Conceivably, the optimal policy is an ad valorem tariff if only ad valorem instruments are available—but it is a specific subsidy if only specific instruments are. As for which of these is better, only explicit calculation can say.

We now turn to more formal analysis. To make the point, we begin by considering the case of a monopolist selling into the domestic market, facing an inverse demand function $p(m)$. When the monopolist faces a specific tariff at a rate t, he sets

$$c^* = p(m) + mp'(m) - t.$$

Now suppose that we replace the specific tariff with an ad valorem tariff that would be equivalent if m were unchanged; that is, tax imports at a rate τ such that

$$\frac{p(m)}{(1 + \tau)} = p(m) - t$$

at the original m. Then the marginal revenue now perceived by the monopolist will be

$$\frac{p(m)}{1 + \tau} + \frac{mp'(m)}{1 + \tau} = p(m) + \frac{mp'(m)}{1 + \tau} - t > c^*.$$

That is, the monopolist will have an incentive to increase sales to the domestic market. So we can always replace a specific tariff with an ad valorem tariff that yields both more imports and better terms of trade.

*Cournot Oligopoly

We can derive the general formula for an optimal ad valorem tariff when there is a homogeneous import. If $m(\tau)$ describes the equilibrium relationship between imports and the tax rate and the demand function is $p(m)$, we obtain $p'm'd\tau = (1 + \tau)dp^* + p^*d\tau$. Substituting these relationships into (2.6) yields

$$U'(\tau) = \left\{ \epsilon_P[m(\tau)] + \frac{m(\tau)}{(1 + \tau)m'(\tau)} \right\} p^*(\tau)m'(\tau) + \tau p^*(\tau)m'(\tau), \qquad (4.9)$$

where $p^*(\tau)$ denotes the import price as a function of the tax rate and $\epsilon_P(\cdot)$ denotes the elasticity of $p(m)$, defined to be positive (equal to the inverse of the elasticity of demand).

To evaluate the desirability of a tax or subsidy policy, we need to know $m'(\tau)$, which depends on conduct and market structure. Consider the case of a Cournot oligopoly with n suppliers. In a symmetrical equilibrium the first-order condition of a representative supplier, which reflects the equality of his perceived marginal revenue to marginal costs, can be written as [compare to (4.4)]

$$\frac{1}{n} MR(m) + \left(1 - \frac{1}{n}\right) p(m) = (1 + \tau)c^*. \qquad (4.10)$$

From here we calculate $m'(\tau)$, which upon substitution into (4.9) yields

$$U'(\tau) = \{\epsilon_P[m(\tau)] - \epsilon_{MR}[m(\tau)]\} \lambda[m(\tau), n]p^*(\tau)m'(\tau) \\ + \tau p^*(\tau)m'(\tau), \qquad (4.11)$$

where $\epsilon_{MR}(\cdot)$ denotes the elasticity of the marginal revenue function, defined to be positive, and

$$\lambda(m,\ n) \equiv \frac{MR(m)/n}{MR(m)/n + [1 - (1/n)]p(m)}\ .$$

Since the first term on the right-hand side of (4.11) represents the terms of trade effect, and $m'(\tau) < 0$, a small ad valorem tariff improves the terms of trade if and only if the elasticity of the marginal revenue curve exceeds the elasticity of the demand curve. This replaces the condition on the relative slopes of these curves in the case of specific taxes. Hence a small ad valorem tariff raises welfare when the demand curve is less elastic than the marginal revenue curve, and a small import subsidy raises welfare when the marginal revenue curve is less elastic.

The optimal tax that satisfies $U'(\tau) = 0$ also satisfies

$$\tau = \{\epsilon_{MR}[m(\tau)] - \epsilon_p[m(\tau)]\}\ \lambda[m(\tau),\ n].$$

Hence optimality calls for a tariff when the elasticity of the marginal revenue curve exceeds the elasticity of the demand curve and a subsidy when the demand curve is more elastic. In the case of a single monopolist $n = 1$, $\lambda(m,\ 1) = 1$, and the optimal ad valorem tax rate equals the difference between the elasticity of the marginal revenue curve and the demand curve. With a larger number of firms the optimal tax rate is smaller in absolute value than the elasticity differential.

Conclusion

An ad valorem tax biases the desirable policy in favor of a tariff relative to a specific tax. The reason is that whenever the marginal revenue curve is steeper than the demand curve the elasticity of the marginal revenue curve exceeds the elasticity of the demand curve (because price exceeds marginal revenue). Hence, whenever it is optimal to impose a specific tariff, it is also optimal to impose an ad valorem tariff. By the same logic, whenever it is optimal to impose an ad valorem import subsidy, it is also optimal to impose a specific import subsidy. The converse, however, does not apply. Namely, the optimal ad valorem policy may be a tax, whereas the optimal specific policy calls for a subsidy.

We do not have to look hard for examples. Simply consider two cases: a demand curve of constant elasticity, and one where the slopes of demand and marginal revenue are always the same. In the first case, as we saw in section 4.2, the optimal specific instrument is a subsidy, but since the elasticity of marginal revenue equals that of demand, the optimal ad valorem policy is a zero tariff. In the second case, the optimal specific policy is a zero subsidy, but the optimal ad valorem policy is a tariff. These examples also show that the optimal instrument may be either specific or ad valorem. The only thing for sure is that an ad valorem subsidy or a specific tariff is never optimal.

4.9 Quotas under Oligopoly

In section 4.3 we delivered a clear negative judgment on quotas in the presence of a foreign monopolist, arguing that such quotas always worsen the terms of trade. The reason is that faced with a quantitative limit on sales, a monopolist will always choose to raise his price to the level that reduces demand to the allowed quantity and will thereby appropriate all of the quota rents.

When there is more than one foreign supplier, this result becomes less certain. In particular, exporters facing a highly restrictive quota may fail to raise their prices sufficiently to clear the market; the result will be the emergence of quota rents that can be appropriated by whoever holds the import licenses. As before, we assume that import licenses are held by domestic residents.

In this section we restrict our attention to the case of Bertrand oligopoly in which firms set prices. The Cournot case presents conceptual difficulties here: if the planned deliveries of all firms combined exceed the quota, who gets rationed and how? In the Bertrand case, by contrast, there is a natural market solution, and we therefore focus on this relatively clear case.

Consider, then, a Bertrand oligopoly of the type discussed in section 4.7. The inverse demand function facing a representative exporter is $p_i = p(m_i, P_i)$, where P_i is the price index of competing goods given by

$$P_i = \Phi(p_1, p_2, \ldots, p_{i-1}, p_{i+1}, \ldots, p_n).$$

This ceteris paribus demand function may also be written with quantity as a function of price, as $m_i = D(p_i, P_i)$. This then allows us to define the pari passu demand curve, which results when all firms move their prices together, as $m = D(p, p)$, with the corresponding inverse being $p = \bar{P}(m)$.

Every producer chooses his own price, taking other prices as given. Let p_i^* be the price chosen by producer i. In the absence of quotas this would also be the domestic price. However, in the presence of a quota the domestic price may differ from the price charged by the exporter, with the difference accruing to owners of quota rights. Suppose that a quota Q applies to the entire group of foreign oligopolists, where we measure Q in physical units.[3] Then competition among owners of quota rights will equalize rent per unit quota. So the difference between the domestic price p_i and the import price p_i^* will be the same for every good, equal to the quota rent R; that is, $R = p_i - p_i^*$ for every i. Naturally, the rent R cannot be negative.

To simplify the exposition, we now deal with a duopoly. In this case $P_1 = p_2$ and $P_2 = p_1$. The equilibrium quota rent as a function of import prices and quota size is determined as follows: If import prices (p_1^*, p_2^*) are such that import demand evaluated at these prices falls short of the quota, the rent equals zero. If, on the other hand, import demand evaluated at import prices exceeds the quota, then the rent satisfies the requirement that import demand at prices $(p_1^* + R, p_2^* + R)$ just equals the quota:

$$D(p_1^* + R, p_2^* + R) + D(p_2^* + R, p_1^* + R) = Q. \qquad (4.11)$$

Let $\rho(p_1^*, p_2^*, Q)$ be the solution of R implicit in (4.11). Then the quota rent is

$$R(p_1^*, p_2^*, Q) = \begin{cases} \rho(p_1^*, p_2^*, Q), & \text{for } \rho(p_1^*, p_2^*, Q) \geq 0, \\ 0 & \text{otherwise.} \end{cases} \qquad (4.12)$$

Two points about $R(\cdot)$ should be apparent. First, the larger the allowed volume of imports, the lower is the quota rent. Second, an increase in either firm's price will, other things equal, reduce the demand for its product more than it raises the demand for the other firm's good, and thus require a decline in R. In particular, a little thought will show that if $p_1 = p_2$ initially, a one-unit rise in either price will lower R by half a unit—that is, $\partial\rho(p^*, p^*, Q)/\partial p_1 = \partial\rho(p^*,$

---

3. This actually poses a conceptual problem, since we assume that products of different firms are imperfect substitutes, and there may be no natural common physical unit of measurement. We assume, however, that these are products like automobiles or shoes for which there is a natural unit that applies to differentiated products—and that there is no quality ranking that would give rise to the "upgrading" effects that often result from quotas in real life (see, for example, Feenstra 1984).

p^*, $Q)/\partial p_2 = -\frac{1}{2}$ for $i = 1$, 2.[4] In addition, when both prices rise by the same amount, the rent falls by this amount.

Foreign exporters are aware of the relationship between their pricing policy and the rent, as described in (4.12). Therefore the perceived demand function of the first exporter is

$$\tilde{D}(p_1^*, p_2^*, Q) \equiv D[p_1^* + R(p_1^*, p_2^*, Q), p_2^* + R(p_1^*, p_2^*, Q)], \qquad (4.13)$$

and analogously for the second exporter.

Now as long as the quota does not bind imports, (4.13) will correspond to the usual ceteris paribus demand function that each producer sees herself as facing under Bertrand competition. In particular, each producer will see two sources of sales gains from a price reduction: a shift in demand away from the other firm, and an increase in overall industry sales.

If the quota is binding, however, an exporter can increase sales only at her competitor's expense. As we have just seen, if one firm cuts its price, there will be a rise in the quota rent that keeps a suitable average price per unit unchanged and thus chokes off any increase in industry sales. Only the increase in sales that results from switching of demand between the competing products is left. The upshot is that the demand curve that each firm sees itself as facing is steeper than the ordinary demand curve in the absence of a quota.[5] We denote by $p_1^* = p^0(m_1, p_2^*, Q)$ the inverse of the perceived demand function given in (4.13).

Figure 4.8 describes the outcome in the absence of a quota. The equilibrium configuration (p_F^*, m_F) is on the pari passu demand curve $\tilde{P}(m_1)$, as described by point 1. The ceteris paribus demand curve $p(m_1, p_F^*)$ also passes through this point. In addition the marginal revenue curve associated with the ceteris paribus demand curve, $MR(m_1, p_F^*) \equiv p(m_1, p_F^*) + m_1 p_m(m_1, p_F^*)$, intersects the marginal cost curve at point 2, which is exactly at the equilibrium quantity. Naturally, the perceived marginal revenue curve $\widetilde{MR}(m_1) \equiv MR[m_1, \tilde{P}(m_1)]$ (not drawn) also passes through point 2.

In examining the effect of an import quota, we begin by considering

---

4. To see this, differentiate (4.11) with respect to p_1 and R to obtain $(D_1 + D_2)dp_1 + (2D_1 + 2D_2)dR = 0$, which implies that $dR = (-\frac{1}{2})dp_1$.

5. This point may be proved, for the case where prices are initially equal, as follows: From the definition of the perceived demand function of the first exporter, we obtain $\tilde{D}_1 = D_1 + (D_1 + D_2)R_1$. When evaluated at equal export prices, $D_1 + D_2 < 0$ from the assumption $0 < p_P(m, P) < 1$ for $P = p(m, P)$, and $R_1 = -\frac{1}{2}$. Hence $-\tilde{D}_1 < -D_1$.

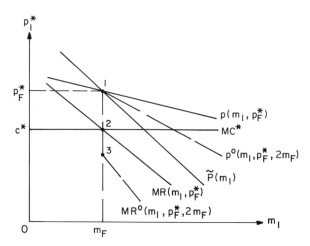

$p(m_1, p_F^*)$

MC^*

$p^0(m_1, p_F^*, 2m_F)$

$\tilde{P}(m_1)$

$MR(m_1, p_F^*)$

$MR^0(m_1, p_F^*, 2m_F)$

Figure 4.8

a quota set at exactly the free trade level of imports—that is, $Q = 2m_F$. Does this induce any change in prices? It is straightforward to see that it does not, by considering the effect of the quota on the ceteris paribus demand curve facing each firm. Suppose that firm 1 were to raise its price. Then overall demand for imports would be reduced, and the quota would not be binding. So to the left of point 1 the demand curve would be unaffected. On the other hand, if firm 1 were to lower its price, the quota would prevent any increase in total imports, and part of the price reduction would be offset by the emergence of a quota rent. So to the right of point 1 the exporter would face a steeper demand curve, as illustrated by the broken line. The overall result, then, is a kinked demand curve. As we have already seen in section 4.5, the marginal revenue that corresponds to such a kinked demand curve is discontinuous: it consists of the solid line to the left of point 2, but the broken line (below the free trade marginal revenue) from point 3 to the right. Clearly, it is not profitable for the firm either to raise or to lower its price: raising its price was unprofitable before imposition of the quota and remains equally unprofitable afterward; lowering its price is less attractive than before.

The discontinuity of marginal revenue now implies, however, that an import quota that is not too restrictive will not generate any rents. To see this, consider figure 4.9. Here we show a quota Q somewhat

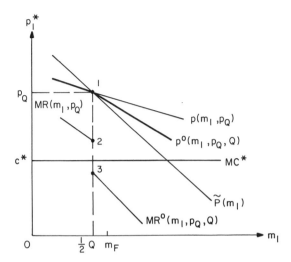

Figure 4.9

smaller than the free trade level $2m_F$. We suppose that both firms charge a price that eliminates any quota rents, $p_Q = \tilde{P}(Q/2)$, and ask whether this is an equilibrium. If the second exporter charges price p_Q, the first exporter's demand curve is the heavy line kinked curve, which consists of the ordinary ceteris paribus demand curve to the left of $Q/2$ and the steeper perceived demand curve to its right. The marginal revenue curve has two corresponding portions and is discontinuous at $Q/2$. We know that when $Q/2 = m_F$, point 2 lies on the marginal cost curve and point 3 well below; so as long as Q is not too far below $2m_F$, point 3 will remain below the marginal cost curve. Hence under these circumstances the first exporter maximizes profits by charging price p_Q and selling half the quota. The same argument applies to the second exporter, which shows that this is indeed an equilibrium. However, since the import price equals the domestic price (because it is read off the pari passu demand curve), quota rents are zero.

We see then, that as long as a quota is not too restrictive point 3 will lie below marginal cost, and foreign firms will raise their prices to capture all quota rents. Obviously, this means that an import quota worsens instead of improving the importing country's terms of trade, and thus leaves it worse off. This is of course exactly what we found in the monopoly case.

When the quota is sufficiently restrictive, however, competition among exporting firms can lead them to set prices that do not squeeze out all rents. The intuition is the following: When a quota becomes highly restrictive, exporting firms find that they sell small quantities at prices that greatly exceed marginal cost. In this situation a firm sees the cost of reducing its price, in terms of lower revenue on existing sales, as low, while the potential gains from additional sales are large—even if these sales must be captured wholly at the expense of rival exporters. So when the allowed volume of imports is small enough, competition drives prices below the level that eliminates rents.

The breakdown of the zero-rent equilibrium is illustrated in figure 4.10, which uses the same representation as figure 4.9. If firm 2 were to charge the rent-eliminating price, p_Q, firm 1 would face the heavy line kinked demand curve passing through point 1. However, marginal revenue is now so high (because of small sales and a high price) that point 3 lies above the marginal cost curve. So the profit-maximizing quantity is at point 4. But this means that both firms want to cut their prices below p_Q.

As firm 2 cuts its price, this will lower firm 1's demand curve, with

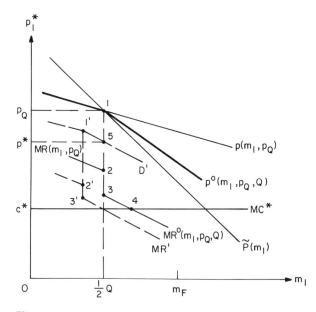

Figure 4.10

the kink moving to the left of $Q/2$. The same will happen to firm 2's demand as firm 1 cuts its price. An equilibrium is attained when the downward shift of the demand curve brings about a downward shift of the marginal revenue curve until it intersects the marginal cost curve at $Q/2$. This is described by the broken line demand and marginal revenue curves; the second exporter's price changes to p^*, point 1 shifts to 1', point 2 to 2', and point 3 to 3'. Now the first exporter finds it profit maximizing to charge price p^*, thereby matching the competitor's price, and to export his pro-rata share of the quota. The same applies to the second exporter, and we have therefore a symmetric equilibrium. Observe, however, that now the import price is not on the pari passu demand curve, implying positive quota rents. The domestic price is on that demand curve, therefore the domestic price equals p_Q, and the quota rent equals the difference between the domestic price and the import price, namely, the vertical distance between points 1 and 5.

Reducing the allowed volume of imports below a certain critical level, then, though it continues to raise the consumer price, will not raise export prices by as much, so that rents to holders of import licenses will emerge. It is indeed possible that restricting imports below the critical level will actually reduce the export price; in this case the improvement in the terms of trade from a more restrictive quota will raise welfare. Thus the costs of a quota may not be monotonic in the quota's restrictiveness: beyond a certain point tightening the quota raises welfare instead of reducing it.[6]

We can confirm this insight with a specific example. In the appendix to this section we calculate the results of an import quota in a market in which two foreign firms each face the demand curve $p(m, P) = A - m + aP$. In this case the critical quota Q_c below which rents are positive is at least two-thirds of the free trade import volume.

The heavy kinked line in figure 4.11 describes the relationship between the equilibrium import price and the quota per commodity; that is, $q \equiv Q/2$. The import price rises with the quota for quotas below the critical level $q_c \equiv Q_c/2$, and falls thereafter, when the import price is on the pari passu demand curve. To evaluate welfare changes that result from changing quota size, consider changing the quota

---

6. See also Eldor and Levin (1987) for a nonmonotonicity result on profits of a domestic monopoly in the presence of voluntary export restraints.

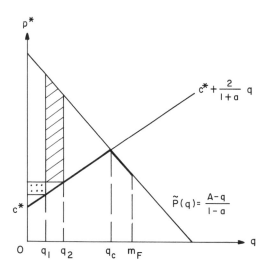

p^*

$$c^* + \frac{2}{1+a}\, q$$

$$\tilde{P}(q) = \frac{A-q}{1-a}$$

c^*

$O \quad q_1 \quad q_2 \quad\quad q_c \quad m_F$

q

Figure 4.11

from q_1 to q_2. As usual we measure welfare by net surplus, which equals the area below the demand curve (here the pari passu demand curve) minus import costs. The proposed quota change increases net surplus by the difference between the lined area and the dotted area. This change raises welfare. It is, in fact, clear from the figure that for small values of q welfare increases with a small enough relaxation of the import restriction. Moreover, applying the same procedure to represent changes in net surplus, we see that for quota levels close to the critical value q_c small relaxations of the import restriction reduce welfare. We show in the appendix to this chapter that there exists a unique level q_x that maximizes welfare in this range. For quotas above the critical level, welfare is higher the less severe the restriction. Hence the relationship between welfare and quota size is as depicted in figure 4.12; it rises for small quotas, declines for an intermediate range, and rises again for high quota values.

Although in this example a small quota is sometimes better than a larger one, free trade is always better still. That is, there are no welfare-improving quotas (see, however, Krishna 1988b for extensions of our argument).

Finally, we should note that the result that making a very restrictive quota still more restrictive may increase welfare depends on including quota rents in domestic welfare—that is, on the assumption that

welfare

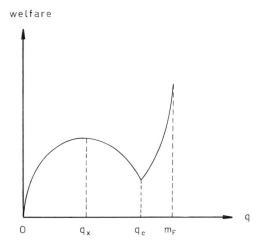

Figure 4.12

import licenses are issued to domestic residents. Clearly, in the case where licenses are, instead, issued to foreigners—whether through a formal "orderly market arrangement," such as the Multi-Fiber Arrangement in textiles and apparel, or a voluntary export restraint agreement, such as in autos, making a quota more restrictive will necessarily worsen the importing country's terms of trade even if the prices charged by the exporting *firms* are reduced. Also, if quota rents are largely dissipated through rent-seeking activities, as suggested by Krueger (1974) and Bhagwati (1982), this will obviate any possibility that tightening a quota brings any gain. Since many quotas are in fact either allocated to residents of exporting countries or the subject of significant rent-seeking expenditures, the prospect that one could actually expect to improve welfare by reducing the quantity of imports allowed needs to be treated with great caution.

4.10* Appendix to Section 4.9

We develop here the linear example discussed in the text. The demand function is

$$p(m, P) = A - m + aP,$$ (4A.1)

where A is a positive constant and a is between zero and one. We also require $A > (1 - a)c^*$. In this case the pari passu demand function is

$$\tilde{P}(m) = \frac{A - m}{1 - a}, \tag{4A.2}$$

and the marginal revenue functions is

$$MR(m, P) = A - 2m + aP. \tag{4A.3}$$

By equating marginal revenue to marginal costs and requiring the price-quantity combination to be on the pari passu demand function, we obtain the free trade price and quantity configuration:

$$p_f = \frac{A + c^*}{2 - a}, \tag{4A.4}$$

$$m_f = \frac{A - (1 - a)c^*}{2 - a}. \tag{4A.5}$$

From (4.11) we calculate $\rho(p_1^*, p_2^*, Q) \equiv (A - Q/2)/(1 - a) - (p_1^* + p_2^*)/2$, which upon substitution into (4.12) and (4.13) yields the perceived demand function for the quota binding region:

$$\tilde{D}(p_1^*, p_2^*, Q) = \frac{1}{2} Q - \frac{1 + a}{2} (p_1^* - p_2^*), \tag{4A.6}$$

with the inverse

$$p^0(m_1, p_2^*, Q) = p_2^* + \frac{1}{1 + a} (Q - 2m_1) \tag{4A.7}$$

and the associated marginal revenue curve

$$MR^0(m_1, p_2^*, Q) = p_2^* + \frac{1}{1 + a} (Q - 4m_1). \tag{4A.8}$$

We calculate the p_Q corresponding to figure 4.9 from the pari passu demand function,

$$p_Q = \frac{A - Q/2}{1 - a}, \tag{4A.9}$$

and use this result to calculate the marginal revenue at point 3 in the figure:

$$MR^0 \left(\frac{Q}{2}, p_Q, Q \right) = \frac{A - Q(3 - a)/(1 + a)}{1 - a}. \tag{4A.10}$$

This value is declining in Q, and there exists therefore a unique quota level at which it equals marginal costs c^*:

$$Q_c = \frac{2[A - (1 - a)c^*](1 + a)}{3 - a} . \tag{4A.11}$$

Hence quotas above this critical level do not generate rents. The magnitude of this critical level is best evaluated as a share of the free trade import volume, which we calculate to be

$$\frac{Q_c}{2m_f} = \frac{(1 + a)(2 - a)}{3 - a} . \tag{4A.12}$$

For a between zero and one, the right-hand side increases in a. Therefore the critical quota is in between two-thirds and one hundred percent of the free trade import volume.

Now we calculate the equilibrium price as a function of quota size in the region in which the quota generates positive rents; that is, $Q \leq Q_c$. In the resulting symmetrical equilibrium every exporter sells $Q/2$ and charges the same price p^*. In addition marginal revenue $MR^0(m, p^*, Q)$ equals marginal costs c^*, as is evident from figure 4.10. Therefore the equilibrium price can be calculated from the relationship $MR^0(Q/2, p^*, Q) = c^*$. From (4A.8) this implies that

$$p^* = c^* + \frac{Q}{1 + a} . \tag{4A.13}$$

This justifies the construction of the price function in figure 4.11.

Next, consider welfare, which we measure by the surplus below the import function minus import costs. Let $q = Q/2$ denote imports per product in the presence of a quota. Then our welfare measure is

$$W(q) = \int_0^q \tilde{P}(m)dm - p^*(q)q,$$

where $p^*(q)$ denote the import price given $q = Q/2$. This measures the net surplus per commodity. Using (4A.2), we calculate

$$W(q) = q\left[\frac{A - q/2}{1 - a} - p^*(q)\right] . \tag{4A.14}$$

For $Q_c/2 \leq q \leq m_f$, import prices are on the pari passu demand function. Therefore

$$W(q) = \frac{q^2}{2(1 - a)} , \qquad \text{for } Q_c/2 \leq q \leq m_f. \tag{4A.15}$$

Hence in this region welfare is higher the larger the quota. For smaller quotas, prices satisfy (4A.13), implying that

$$W(q) = \frac{q[A - (1 - a)c^* - q(5 - 3a)/2(1 + a)]}{1 - a} , \tag{4A.16}$$

for $0 \le q \le Q_c/2$.

In this case welfare increases, reaching a peak, and then declines in q, as depicted in figure 4.12. We calculate the welfare-maximizing quota in this region by solving $W'(q) = 0$, which implies that

$$q_x = \frac{[A - (1 - a)c^*](1 + a)}{5 - 3a} . \tag{4A.17}$$

In order to see whether there exists a quota that improves welfare, it is sufficient to compare $W(m_f)$ with $W(q_x)$. Using (4A.5) with (4A.15) and (4A.17) with (4A.16) implies that

$$\frac{W(q_x)}{W(m_f)} = \frac{(1 + a)(2 - a)^2}{5 - 3a} . \tag{4A.18}$$

For a between zero and one, the right-hand side declines in a. For $a = 0$, it equals 4/5, and it approaches 1 as a approaches 1. Hence in the linear case free trade dominates every quota.

References

Bhagwati, Jagdish N. (1982). "Directly unproductive, profit-seeking (DUP) activities." *Journal of Political Economy* 90: 988–1002.

Brander, James A., and Spencer, Barbara J. (1981). "Tariffs and the extraction of foreign monopoly rents under potential entry." *Canadian Journal of Economics* 14: 371–389.

Brander, James A., and Spencer, Barbara J. (1984a). "Tariff protection and imperfect competition." In Henryk Kierzkowski (ed.), *Monopolistic Competition and International Trade*. Oxford: Blackwell.

Brander, James A., and Spencer, Barbara J. (1984b). "Trade warfare: Tariffs and cartels." *Journal of International Economics* 16: 227–242.

Eldor, Rafael, and Levin, Dan (1987). "Trade liberalization and imperfect competition: A welfare analysis." The Foerder Institute for Economic Research. Working Paper No. 18-87.

Feenstra, Robert (1984). "Voluntary export restraint in U.S. autos, 1980–81: quality, employment, and welfare effects." In Robert E. Baldwin and Anne O. Krueger (eds.), *The Structure and Evolution of Recent U.S. Trade Policies*. Chicago: University of Chicago Press.

Jones, Ronald W. (1987). "Trade taxes and subsidies with imperfect competition." *Economics Letters* 23: 375–379.

Krishna, Kala (1988a). "The case of the vanishing revenues: Auction quotas with monopoly." Mimeo.

Krishna, Kala (1988b). "The case of the vanishing revenues: Auction quotas with oligopoly." Mimeo.

Krueger, Anne O. (1974). "The political economy of the rent-seeking society." *American Economic Review* 64: 291–303.

Shibata, Hirofumi (1968). "A note on the equivalence of tariffs and quotas." *American Economic Review* 58: 137–142.

5

Strategic Export Policy

In the last two chapters we considered situations of one-sided market power—that is, situations in which either domestic or foreign firms are imperfectly competitive, but there is no rivalry between oligopolists based in different countries. In this chapter we finally turn to the case of two-sided market power.

As one might expect, introducing market power on both sides also introduces a new issue: the possibility of *strategic* trade policy. In general, strategic moves may be defined as actions that by themselves are not desirable but that alter the behavior of others in ways that work to the strategic player's advantage. The classic example from industrial organization is investment in excess capacity by a firm in order to deter entry by new competitors: the excess capacity viewed in isolation lowers the firm's profits, but the effect on the behavior of firms that would otherwise have entered makes the expense worthwhile. In the trade policy context, the now-standard example is that of an export subsidy that would ordinarily lower national welfare but that may raise welfare if it has a deterrent effect on foreign competition.

In order to focus clearly on the strategic aspects of trade policy, for most of this chapter we will restrict the domain of international competition by assuming that domestic and foreign firms are competing over the market for a good for which there is no domestic demand. This assumption sets aside most of the issues we discussed in the last two chapters; imports cannot affect the degree of competition in the domestic market, and trade policy cannot be used to extract lower prices from foreign suppliers. The result is to focus all of our attention on the competition between domestic and foreign firms, making the strategic aspects of trade policy central.

It is worth emphasizing the artificiality of this setup. In real life the effects of trade policy on domestic consumers are crucial; a model that neglects these effects in order to focus on the competition between firms may be useful in isolating some interesting effects but is a terrible guide to policy. This is important because, as we will see, the simplest model of strategic export policy provides a result that bears a superficial resemblance to crude mercantilist views. Under certain very specific conditions a government policy of subsidizing exports can act as a strategic move that, by tilting international competition in favor of domestic firms, raises national welfare at other countries' expense. The seductive appeal of this result is clearly apparent. What we need to understand from the outset is that the result is not a vindication of the popular view that sees international trade as a zero-sum game in which the most aggressive governments win. Even in the context of pure export competition the case for strategic export promotion needs to be severely qualified; when we turn to more complete models, little of the apparent support for mercantilism will remain.

As a way of placing the case for strategic export policies in context, we begin with the nonstrategic case of a country that simply faces a downward-sloping demand curve for its exports. We then turn to strategic interaction, showing how the appropriate role of the government depends on both the market structure and the conduct of firms. Adding to the complexity are the effects of entry by new firms, general equilibrium effects, and strategic interaction among governments; we consider each in turn. Finally, we conclude by relaxing the assumption that competition takes place only in the export market.

5.1 Competitive Foreign Conduct

The principal concern of this chapter will be the effects of export policy in a world where both domestic and foreign firms are imperfectly competitive. However, as a first step it is useful to consider the potential for an active export policy in a world where foreign firms behave competitively.

When foreign firms act as atomistic competitors, the world environment facing a domestic industry may be summarized by a downward-sloping demand curve that embodies the responses of both the foreign firms (increasing their sales as the price rises) and foreign consumers. Such an export demand curve is shown as D in figure 5.1.

Now in chapter 2 we already analyzed the optimal trade policy when the domestic industry is perfectly competitive. We repeat this analysis briefly, assuming constant marginal costs. In figure 5.1 MC represents the domestic industry's marginal cost curve; in the absence of domestic consumers and with price-taking behavior by domestic firms, it is also the export supply curve. The intersection of the demand and marginal cost curves at point 1 determines the free trade exports and price.

The optimal restriction of exports occurs where marginal revenue MR intersects the marginal cost curve; that is, at point 2. Optimal exports are X_M, and foreigners should be charged price p_M. With competitive domestic suppliers this goal can be achieved by imposing an export tax equal to the vertical distance between points 2 and 3.

What is now immediately apparent is that the same result can be achieved without government intervention when the domestic export industry is monopolized by a single firm or when there are a number of domestic firms acting as a profit-maximizing cartel. In either case the industry will set marginal revenue equal to marginal cost, achieving the same export price as an optimal export tax—except that tax revenue accrues as profits, instead. We will see later that an export monopoly is not the same as an optimal tax when there is domestic

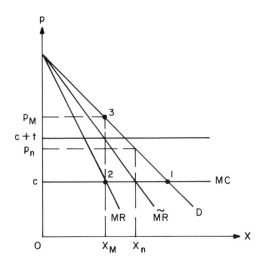

Figure 5.1

consumption of the export good. At this stage the important point to notice, however, is that as long as the foreign industry is perfectly competitive, there is no case for export subsidy. At best a laissez-faire policy is optimal when there is a domestic monopolist; an export *tax* is welfare improving when the domestic industry is competitive.

Of course the cases of monopoly and perfect competition do not span the full range of possibilities. Sometimes imperfectly competitive industries can give rise to behavior that has no counterpart in either of the polar cases of perfect competition and monopoly. However, in this case noncooperative oligopoly does lead to a case for export taxes rather than subsidies, in the same way as does perfect competition.

Consider first an industry composed of n identical firms that compete in Cournot fashion. We saw in chapter 3 that the Cournot equilibrium output is characterized by equality of the perceived marginal revenue $\widetilde{MR}(X, n) \equiv (1 - 1/n)p(X) + (1/n)MR(X)$ and marginal costs. Thus a representative firm's perceived marginal revenue is a weighted average of the inverse demand function $p(X)$ and its associated marginal revenue function $MR(X)$, where the weights depend on the degree of concentration. The more firms there are in the industry the closer is the perceived marginal revenue curve to the demand curve. Figure 5.1 describes a situation in which marginal costs are constant. It is optimal to export X_M and to charge foreigners price p_M. The perceived marginal revenue curve is drawn on the assumption that the number of firms is at least 2 and finite. Equilibrium output equals X_n, and equilibrium price equals p_n. Clearly, the oligopoly exports too much and charges a price that is too low.

We can induce the oligopoly to choose the optimal price-quantity combination by imposing a suitable export tax. Suppose that the export tax equals t per unit exported. We employ a specific tax, but in this case it does not matter whether the tax is specific or ad valorem (because profits are part of the economy's surplus). The tax is optimal if the tax-inclusive marginal cost curve intersects the perceived marginal revenue curve at exports X_M, as drawn in the figure. Since the perceived marginal revenue curve is closer to the demand curve the larger the number of firms, *the optimal tax is higher the larger the number of firms*.

To understand the nature of this optimal tax, we relate it to the underlying fundamentals. The optimal tax equals $t = \widetilde{MR}(X_M) - c$ (see figure 5.1). However, since true marginal revenue equals marginal costs at this output level, we also have $t = \widetilde{MR}(X_M) - MR(X_M)$. That is the optimal tax equals the difference between perceived and true marginal revenue, which can also be represented as

$$t = -p'(X_M)(n - 1)\left(\frac{X_M}{n}\right). \tag{5.3}$$

This formula has a standard externality interpretation. When a single firm considers expanding output by one unit, its revenue increases by the price minus revenue lost on inframarginal sales. Thus its marginal revenue equals $p(X_M) + x_M p'(X_M)$, where $x_M = X_M/n$ denotes its sales in a symmetrical equilibrium. However, the price decline also reduces revenue of other firms in the industry. The latter is not taken into account by the representative firm, but counts in national welfare. Therefore the negative externality is valued at $(n - 1)(X_M/n)p'(X_M)$, and the optimal tax equals the negative externality.

The nature of the optimal policy and its basic characterization do not change when firms produce imperfect substitutes and play Bertrand rather than Cournot. This we demonstrate in figure 5.2, in which we have drawn the pari passu demand curve $\bar{P}(x)$, where x denotes output of a single firm. The associated true marginal revenue curve $MR(x) \equiv \bar{P}(x) + x\bar{P}'(x)$ differs from the *perceived* marginal revenue curve $\widetilde{MR}(x) \equiv \bar{P}(x) + xp_x[x, \bar{P}(x)]$; the latter lies everywhere

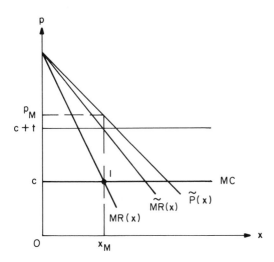

Figure 5.2

above the former (although below the demand curve).[1] The reason is that the same kind of externality is present as in the Cournot case. A firm that increases sales by lowering its price fails to take into account the fact that by so doing, it cuts into other firms' sales and profits; it therefore perceives a higher marginal revenue from unilateral action than is in fact true for the industry as a whole. Optimal exports may be found in the usual way by equating marginal costs to true marginal revenue, as at point 1. Optimal exports per firm are thus x_M, and the optimal price equals p_M. Since the perceived marginal revenue curve is above MR, however, oligopolistic competition will lead to exports that are too large and prices that are too low, just as in the Cournot case. An optimal export tax is therefore indicated in order to raise the tax-inclusive marginal cost curve until it intersects the perceived marginal revenue curve at exports x_M. Evidently, the optimal tax per unit equals the difference between perceived marginal revenue and true marginal revenue:

$$t = \widetilde{MR}(x_M) - MR(x_M),$$

where the difference measures the externality imposed by a single firm on its domestic competitors (see Dixit 1984, who also discusses antitrust policies).

Clearly, the case where a domestic industry faces a perfectly competitive foreign industry does not lend support to the idea of subsidized export promotion. Indeed, except in the polar case of a domestic monopolist, the optimal policy is an export *tax* that improves the exporting country's terms of trade. The most famous insight of the strategic trade policy argument is that this may change when the foreign industry is imperfectly competitive.

5.2 Profit Shifting

We now begin our consideration of export policies when a domestic oligopoly faces noncompetitive foreign firms. We begin with the simplest case of a Cournot duopoly consisting of a domestic and a foreign firm. This case is not only simple; it also yields results that are not robust to changes in the economic environment, which we explain in the following sections. As in the previous section, we

---

1. The relative location of the marginal revenue curves stems from the fact that $\tilde{P}'(x) = p_x[x, \tilde{P}(x)]/\{1 - p_P[x, \tilde{P}(x)]\} < p_x[x, \tilde{P}(x)] < 0.$

maintain the assumption that the exported good is not used domestically.

The domestic firm chooses exports x to maximize profits

$$\pi(x, x^*, c) \equiv [p(x + x^*) - c]x,$$

where $p(\cdot)$ is the inverse demand function for the homogeneous product, x^* stands for sales of the foreign firm, and c denotes marginal costs, which are taken to be fixed. As usual, under Cournot conduct each firm takes as given its rival's sales and finds its best response by equating marginal revenue to marginal costs. By solving for profit-maximizing exports as a function of foreign sales, we obtain the reaction function $x = \rho(x^*, c)$. We assume that the reaction function is downward sloping in the relevant range and that the absolute value of the slope is smaller than one; that is, $-1 < \rho_x(x^*, c) < 0.$[2] The foreign firm's reaction function $\rho^*(x, c^*)$ is derived in a similar way, where c^* denotes its fixed marginal cost. We assume that the foreign reaction curve also slopes downward, with a slope smaller than one.

Figure 5.3 presents the resulting equilibrium, which we identify

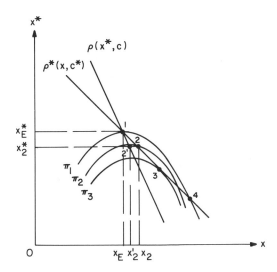

Figure 5.3

2. Linear demand functions satisfy this condition because they imply reaction functions with slope $-\frac{1}{2}$. On the other hand, constant elasticity demand functions imply reaction functions with an upward sloping portion close to the axis of the reacting firm.

by the intersection of the reaction curves at point 1. The home firm exports x_E, and the foreign firm sells x_E^*. We have also drawn a family of isoprofit curves of the home-country firm $\pi(x, x^*, c) = \pi_i$. Since the reaction curve is a locus of points at which profits are maximized for given sales of the rival, the isoprofit curves are flat at their intersection points with the reaction curve. For this reason the iso-profit curve through point 1 lies above the foreign firm's reaction curve immediately to the right of point 1.

The firms could do better by jointly cutting back sales; the duopoly produces more than the joint profit-maximizing quantity. However, as long as there is no cooperation and each firm takes the output of the other as given, they are stuck with the equilibrium at point 1.

Is there anything the domestic firm can do to improve on this outcome? The answer is yes if it can commit itself to export more than x_E. This is easily seen from the figure. Suppose, for example, that the domestic firm can commit itself to export x_2. Then the foreign firm's best response is with sales x_2^*. The domestic firm's profit level rises from π_1 to π_2 (lower isoprofit curves represent higher profit levels). A simple announcement by the domestic firm that it intends to produce x_2 will not do the trick, however. The foreign firm knows that once it chooses sales x_2^*, the domestic firm will have an incentive to produce, not x_2, but x_2', because at point 2' its profits are the largest given x_2^*. Hence, without some precommitment mechanism, a declaration by the domestic firm that it will produce x_2 is not credible. The only credible announcement is that the firm will produce x_E because this is the quantity that it will find profit maximizing after the fact. So point 2 is not an equilibrium; only point 1 is.

Clearly, it would be to the firm's advantage to have some way to precommit itself. Since we have set up our scenario in such a way that the firm's profits equal the nation's gains from exporting, it is in the national interest to provide such a precommitment mechanism if possible. What Brander and Spencer (1985) have pointed out is that export subsidies provide just that. They work as follows. Having the first move advantage (which is questionable in some circumstances but crucial for the argument), the government precommits itself to provide a specific export subsidy s *before* firms make their choices.[3]

---

3. In some circumstances the government does not have the first move advantage. Often firms have to build production facilities, which takes time, and base their decisions on *expected* government policies, such as the availability of export subsidies. They cannot be sure what policies will prevail when their productive capacity will

In this case the firm's marginal costs of exports decline to $c - s$, and it maximizes the subsidy inclusive profits $\pi(x, x^*, c - s)$. Its reaction function becomes $\rho(x^*, c - s)$. Since the reaction function declines in marginal costs, an export subsidy shifts the reaction curve to the right, as depicted in figure 5.4. The equilibrium shifts from 1 to 1'.

The subsidy raises the firm's profits, which include the subsidy. Of course profits accounted for by the subsidy itself are not a net national gain but rather a transfer from taxpayers to the exporting firm. A small subsidy, however, will raise profits by more than the value of the subsidy itself because it will raise the subsidy exclusive profits $\pi(x, x^*, c)$. For example, there exists a subsidy level that will make point 1' in figure 5.4 coincide with point 2 in figure 5.3. At the latter point subsidy-exclusive profits are higher than at point 1. A carefully engineered subsidy can also make the equilibrium point coincide with 3 in figure 5.3, which represents the exporting country's best outcome under this scheme. This is the point that would have been reached if the domestic firm had been a Stackelberg leader.[4]

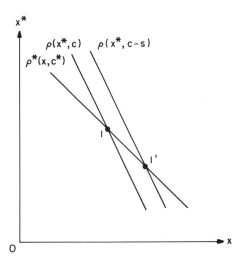

Figure 5.4

become usable, even when the government promises a particular policy. For example, the current government may not be in power at that time. In addition, once the plant exists the incentive to implement a policy may change (this is an example of a time consistency problem). When the firms move first and the government moves second, the nature of the optimal policy may change (see Carmichael 1987; Gruenspecht 1988). Hence the sequencing of decisions plays an important role.
4. A firm is a Stackelberg leader when it has the first move advantage, and it can

We conclude that in this simple model export promotion is beneficial (although excessive export promotion, which moves the equilibrium point to the right of 4 in figure 5.3, is harmful).

On the face of it, this result seems to lend itself to a sort of neo-mercantilist interpretation: the country benefits because its government helps its export industry in competition with a foreign rival. Notice that the profit increase of the domestic firm is associated with a decline in the profits of its foreign rival. Thus in this case the gains from export subsidy may be said to arise from shifting profits from the foreign to the domestic firm.

It seems to us, however, that it is fundamentally misleading to emphasize the profit-shifting aspect of the case for export promotion because it is very specific to the underlying market structure and conduct. The fact is that there are circumstances in which trade policies are beneficial without shifting profits from foreign to domestic firms, as we will show at a later stage. There exists nevertheless a common explanation to the effectiveness of all these policies, and we wish to emphasize this common element.

The key point is that in this case trade intervention is justified by a divergence of private marginal revenue from social marginal revenue whenever the government can act first and precommit to a policy. An optimal export policy—tax or subsidy—closes this gap. That is, the issue is best seen as a kind of domestic divergence rather than specifically as a competitive action vis-à-vis foreigners.

To see this, let us present the same case for export promotion in a different way. Let $p^d(x, x^*) \equiv p(x + x^*)$ denote the demand function facing the domestic firm for a given level of foreign sales. This may be viewed as an "ex post" demand function, one that applies after the foreign firm has chosen its level of sales. The corresponding marginal revenue function is $MR^d(x, x^*) \equiv p^d(x, x^*) + xp_x^d(x, x^*)$. Both are drawn in figure 5.5. In Cournot competition the firm equates marginal revenue for a given level of foreign sales to marginal costs. Therefore point 1 represents its response to foreign sales x^*. If $x^* = x_E^*$, point 1 also represents the duopoly equilibrium point.

The usefulness of policy derives from the inability of the domestic firm to precommit to other levels of exports, thereby preventing it

---

precommit to its choice. In the current context a Stackelberg leader anticipates its rival's response along the rival's reaction curve. For this reason the leader chooses his welfare-maximizing point on the rival's reaction curve.

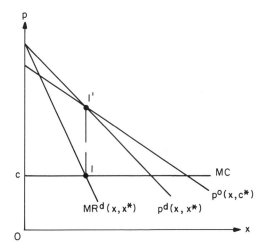

Figure 5.5

from responding to the "ex ante" demand function that takes account of the effect of domestic sales on foreign. This ex ante demand function may be defined as $p^o(x, c^*) \equiv p[x + \rho^*(x, c^*)]$. This is the "true" demand function that a first-moving actor faces; the fact that the firm's decisions are not based on the true demand in this sense is the source of the market failure that government policy can remedy.

We identify the nature of the remedy as follows: By definition, when $x^* = x_E^*$, the ex ante demand curve intersects the ex post demand curve at point 1', which lies vertically above 1.[5] The ex ante demand curve is more elastic (flatter), however, because an increase in the domestic firm's sales, if committed to in advance, will be partly matched by offsetting reductions in the foreign firm's sales and will therefore lower the price by less than what a Cournot firm assumes (because a Cournot firm takes the output of rivals as given).[6] For this reason the true marginal revenue curve passes above point 1. The intersection of the true marginal revenue curve MR^o (not drawn in figure 5.5) with the marginal cost curve determines optimal exports.

---

5. More generally, for every x^* the demand curves $p^o(x, c^*)$ and $p^d(x, x^*)$ intersect at x', which satisfies $x^* = \rho^*(x', c^*)$.

6. By definition, at this point $p_x^o(x_E, c^*) = p'(x_E + x_E^*)[1 + \rho_x^*(x_E, c^*)]$ and $p_x^d(x_E, x_E^*) = p'(x_E + x_E^*)$. Therefore the true demand curve is flatter and downward sloping, as long as the foreign reaction function is downward sloping and its slope is smaller than 1.

Since this curve passes above point 1, equilibrium exports are too low.

Figure 5.6 presents the ex ante demand and marginal revenue curves. Optimal exports are determined at the intersection point 3, which corresponds to point 3 in figure 5.3. Points 1 and 1' from figure 5.5 are also reproduced. Since true marginal revenue is above marginal costs for all export levels between points 1 and 3, all these export levels are more desirable than x_E.

Now suppose that the government wants to induce the domestic firm to export x_3, corresponding to point 3. If it succeeds, foreigners will sell $x_3^* = \rho^*(x_3, c^*)$, which is smaller than x_E^*. A reduction in foreign sales shifts the domestic firm's demand curve to the right, exactly by the decline in foreign sales. Foreign sales decline until the rightward shift makes the firm's demand curve intersect the true demand curve at point 3'. This we represent by the broken line demand curve. The latter is necessarily less elastic than the true demand curve at point 3' (see argument in note 6). For this reason the associated broken line marginal revenue curve passes below the true marginal revenue curve at exports x_3. This representation identifies the optimal policy. Since the domestic firm equates marginal revenue to marginal costs, a reduction of marginal costs to point 3" will induce it to expand exports to the desired level (and the foreign firm to respond with x_3^*). A specific export subsidy s, as pointed out

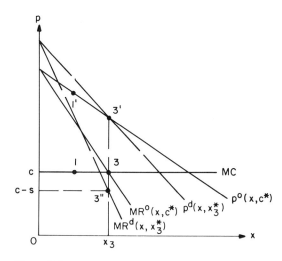

Figure 5.6

in the figure, achieves this goal. It is also clear that every export subsidy smaller than s raises welfare above the free trade level. The optimal subsidy brings private marginal revenue inclusive of subsidy, $MR^d + s$, in line with true social marginal revenue. The optimal subsidy equals the difference between true and perceived marginal revenue:

$$s = MR^o(x_3, c^*) - MR^d(x_3, x_3^*).$$

Using the definitions of the marginal revenue functions, the optimal subsidy can also be expressed in terms of fundamentals as

$$s = x_3 p'(x_3 + x_3^*) \rho_x^*(x_3, c^*). \tag{5.2}$$

The right-hand side represents the effect on revenue of a marginal increase in exports that the domestic firm does not take into account. When the domestic firm considers expanding exports, it assumes that foreign sales do not respond to its decision, when in fact they do. Export expansion by one unit reduces foreign sales by $-\rho_x^*$ units, thereby raising price by $p'\rho_x^*$ units. The price rise times initial exports represents the marginal revenue that the firm disregards. The optimal export subsidy internalizes this element.

The justification for an export subsidy in the case of imperfectly competitive foreigners, then, is that when the domestic firm is unable to precommit, it faces a perceived marginal revenue that lies below the true marginal revenue curve, leading it to underexport. However, we saw in the previous section that when there are several domestic firms facing competitive foreign firms the perceived marginal revenue exceeds the true MR, leading to overexporting and a case for an export *tax*. It seems apparent that when there are both imperfect competitors abroad and several firms at home, these two effects will pull in opposite directions: either an export subsidy or a tax may be indicated.

The first thing to observe is that from the point of view of the country that considers export promotion, the number of foreign firms is of no direct interest; what matters is the foreigners' response to its exports. What also matters is the domestic firms' treatment of foreign sales: Do they consider them to be constant, or do they take into account their response to domestic exports? When foreign suppliers constitute a competitive fringe, their response is internalized in the derived demand function for home exports. This may not be the case when foreign oligopolistic firms occupy the industry. These clarifications suggest the following approach. Let each domestic firm maximize profits, taking as given the output levels of *all* its competitors, domestic and foreign alike. Then we can represent the level of its perceived marginal revenue in a symmetrical equilibrium by

$$MR^{d}(X, X^*) \equiv p(X + X^*) + \left(\frac{X}{n}\right) p'(X + X^*),$$

where X denotes total exports, X^* represents total foreign sales, and n denotes the number of domestic firms. Exports per domestic firm equal X/n. Every firm equates this marginal revenue to the export tax or subsidy inclusive marginal costs. Thus

$$MR^{d}(X, X^*) = c + t - s. \tag{5.3a}$$

Next, let $X^* = \rho^*(X)$ represent foreign sales in response to domestic exports. It depends on the degree of concentration of foreign firms and cost structure. These are taken to be constant. Then $p^{o}(X) \equiv p[X + \rho^*(X)]$ represents the true demand function facing the domestic economy and $MR^{o}(X) \equiv p[X + \rho^*(X)] + Xp'[X + \rho^*(X)][1 + \rho_X^*(X)]$ represents true marginal revenue. Optimal exports X_o are characterized by

$$MR^{o}(X_o) = c. \tag{5.3b}$$

Using $X_o^* = \rho^*(X_o)$ to denote foreign sales at this optimum, a comparison of (5.3a) with (5.3b) shows that the optimal tax subsidy combination satisfies

$$s - t = MR^{o}(X_o) - MR^{d}(X_o, X_o^*).$$

Namely, the net subsidy to exports equals the difference between true and perceived marginal revenue. The definitions of the marginal revenue functions imply that

$$s - t = [X_o p'(X_o + X_o^*)\rho_X^*(X_o)] - \left[-(n - 1)\left(\frac{X_o}{n}\right) p'(X_o + X_o^*)\right]. \tag{5.4}$$

The term in the first set of brackets represents the subsidy called for as a result of the fact that domestic firms do not take into account the response of foreigners to their exports and the effect it has on the profitability of the domestic industry. This is the strategic element in the optimal policy, representing the analog of (5.2). The term in the second set of brackets represents the tax called for as a result of the fact that a typical domestic firm does not take into account the effect of its actions on the profitability of other domestic firms via the direct effect of its output on price (there also exists an indirect effect that is captured in the first term). This element is analogous to (5.1). What is then the nature of the optimal policy? Clearly, it depends on the slope of the foreign reaction curve and on the degree of concentration of the domestic industry. The stronger the foreign response to domestic marginal exports, the more likely it is that export promotion raises welfare. On the other hand, the less concentrated the domestic industry, the more likely it is that export discouragement raises welfare. A necessary and sufficient condition for desirable export promotion (net subsidy) is

$$-\rho_X^*(X_o) > 1 - \frac{1}{n.}$$

Export promotion raises welfare in the presence of a single domestic firm, but reduces welfare in the presence of a sufficiently large number of domestic firms (see Krishna and Thursby 1988 for a more general treatment of this point).

We see, then, that the case for export promotion is not at all well described by the simple idea that domestic firms will prevail in competition if they are given a helping hand by the government. Instead, it turns on a subtle divergence between actual and perceived marginal revenue, one that may easily be reversed even in the most favorable circumstances of market structure and behavior. And as we will see next, plausible alternative models of behavior do not provide any support for export subsidy.

5.3 Price Competition

In a Cournot market the optimal export policy is ambiguous: the potential strategic role of government policy militates toward subsidy, but the externality aspect of competition among domestic firms pushes us toward an export tax. This seems to suggest that at any rate an export subsidy will be optimal if the domestic industry is sufficiently concentrated (where sufficiency may mean pure monopoly). Unfortunately, we cannot even be sure of this. The reason is that the results are sensitive to the character of competition. Whereas export subsidies are sometimes desirable in a Cournot market, they are never desirable in a Bertrand market.

We begin with the argument, originally due to Eaton and Grossman (1986), that even in a duopoly setting Bertrand competition implies that an export tax rather than a subsidy is the appropriate strategic policy.

As usual, let $D(p, p^*)$ represent the demand function facing a domestic exporter who competes with a foreign substitute for his product.[7] We denote his profit function by $\pi(p, p^*, c) \equiv (p - c)D(p, p^*)$. He chooses the price so as to maximize profits, taking as given the price of the competing good. The first-order condition $\pi_1(p, p^*, c) = 0$ implicitly defines his reaction function $\rho(p^*, c)$, which we assume to be rising in foreign price, as described by the upward-sloping reaction curve in figure 5.7.[8] A similar procedure can be used to derive the foreign firm's reaction function $\rho^*(p, c^*)$, also described in the figure. In fact, for current purposes, the foreign reaction curve can be thought of as describing a price index of foreign competing goods as a function of the domestic price, whatever the foreign

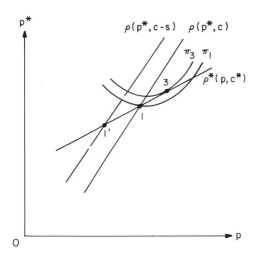

Figure 5.7

7. The usual assumptions on this function are $D_1 < 0$, $D_2 > 0$, and $D_1 + D_2 < 0$. The last assumption states that a proportional increase in the price of both goods reduces demand.
8. Bertrand conduct most likely gives rise to upward-sloping reaction curves for substitute products, whereas Cournot conduct most likely gives rise to downward-sloping reaction curves, although in both cases exceptions are possible. We do not deal with the exceptions.

market structure, as long as the domestic exporter treats this index as given. Naturally, this interpretation restricts the applicability of our analysis to circumstances in which it is reasonable to expect the domestic exporter to treat foreign prices as given.

The intersection of the two reaction curves at point 1 determines equilibrium prices. We assume that the domestic reaction curve is steeper than the foreign reaction curve. The figure also shows iso-profit curves $\pi(p, p^*, c) = \pi_i$. These curves are flat at their intersection points with the domestic reaction curve, and higher isoprofit curves correspond to higher profit levels (because a higher foreign price raises the demand facing the domestic exporter). For this reason there exist points on the foreign reaction curve, to the right of 1, at which domestic profits are higher. Profits are highest at point 3. Therefore the exporter and the exporting country would like to move closer to 3. The exporter cannot do this on his own, however, because he is unable to precommit to a price off his reaction curve. This is where the government comes in; it can use its first mover advantage to alter his incentives.

But what is the right policy? An export subsidy turns out to be precisely the wrong thing to do. Such a subsidy changes the export-er's first-order condition to $\pi_1(p, p^*, c - s) = 0$. Therefore the relevant reaction function becomes $\rho(p^*, c - s)$. Since the reaction function declines with marginal costs, an export subsidy shifts the reaction curve to the left, as drawn in the figure. Hence in this case an export subsidy is harmful; it brings about a reduction of equilibrium prices that are too low for profit to be maximized in the first place. In the duopoly case it hurts the foreign firm as well. This point is best seen by observing that profit levels decline as one moves on a reaction curve closer to the origin.

Clearly, then, the best policy is the reverse: a tax on domestic exports. A tax shifts the domestic reaction curve to the right and the equilibrium point closer to 3. In effect, an export tax allows the domestic firm to credibly commit itself not to be aggressive and to charge a price that raises the profits of both firms. Notice that al-though this is just as much a "strategic" policy as the export subsidy considered earlier, in this case it works to the advantage rather than the disadvantage of the targets of the strategic move. There is no profit shifting here; instead, both exporters gain at the expense of the consumers.

These results represent a special case of a more general point concerning strategic policies. It has been pointed out in the industrial organization literature (see Tirole 1988, ch. 8) that whether it pays to be aggressive or inoffensive in the first stage of a competitive game, at which an irreversible decision is made, depends on whether in the second stage the choice variables are strategic substitutes or complements. Strategic substitution and complementarity are defined so as to coincide with the slopes of the reaction curves: upward-sloping curves represent complements, and downward-sloping curves represent substitutes. In our cases it pays to be aggressive and to subsidize exports in the first stage if the two firms play Cournot in the second stage and the choice variables are strategic substitutes, whereas it pays to be inoffensive, or rather helpful, to the rival in the first stage if they play Bertrand in the second stage and the choice variables are strategic complements.

The case for export taxation can also be explained in terms of the difference between perceived and true demand and marginal revenue curves. In figure 5.8, $p^d(x, p^*)$ represents the inverse of the demand function $D(p, p^*)$, and $MR^d(x, p^*) \equiv p^d(x, p^*) + x p_x^d(x, p^*)$ represents its associated marginal revenue function, both drawn for a particular value $p^* = p_1^*$. Given the price of the foreign substitute product, the domestic exporter equates his perceived marginal revenue $MR^d(x, p^*)$ to marginal costs, as at point 1. He chooses price p_1. By repeating this procedure for all values of p^*, we can trace out his reaction function.

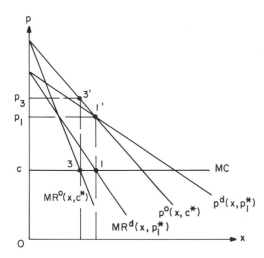

Figure 5.8

To examine the deviation of the resulting equilibrium from the economy's optimum, we construct the true demand function, implicitly defined by $x = D[p, \rho^*(p, c^*)]$. Point 1' in the figure lies on this demand function only if $p_1^* = \rho^*(p_1, c^*)$. Naturally, for the equilibrium value of the foreign price the perceived and true demand functions intersect at the equilibrium domestic price. Suppose that indeed p_1 and p_1^* are equilibrium prices. Then the inverse of the true demand function, denoted by $p^o(x, c^*)$, passes through point 1'. Assuming that it slopes downward, it is necessarily steeper than the perceived demand curve, as depicted in the figure. The relative slopes are apparent from the implicit definition $x = D[p, \rho^*(p, c^*)]$. When the price of the domestic good rises, demand falls as a result of the own price effect. This is also the decline in demand perceived by the exporter. The true demand, however, takes also into account the fact that the foreign price will rise in response to the domestic price increase, thereby raising demand to some extent. Hence the perceived decline in demand exceeds the true one, implying that the perceived demand curve is flatter.

The fact that the perceived demand curve is more elastic than the true one implies that true marginal revenue is below point 1. Optimal exports are found by equating true marginal revenue to marginal costs. Hence, as long as the true marginal revenue curve slopes downward, the optimal point 3 lies to the left of 1. The optimal price equals p_3. Clearly, exports are too large in the initial equilibrium and the price is too low. By comparing figures 5.5 and 5.8, we can see the difference between Cournot and Bertrand conduct. In Cournot the true demand curve is more elastic than the perceived one, whereas in Bertrand it is less elastic. For this reason strategic considerations have opposite implications for optimal trade policy; they call for export subsidies in the Cournot case and for taxation of exports in the Bertrand case.

Figure 5.9 presents the optimal tax. The figure reproduces the true demand and marginal revenue curves, the marginal cost curve, and points 1, 1', 3, and 3' from figure 5.8. If the domestic exporter charges p_3, the foreign price equals $p_3^* = \rho^*(p_3, c^*)$. The perceived demand curve corresponding to this price passes through point 3', as drawn in the figure. It is flatter than the true demand curve and its marginal revenue curve is therefore above point 3. This can be supported as an equilibrium outcome by imposing a tax t on exports such that the tax-inclusive marginal revenue passes through point 3''. With this

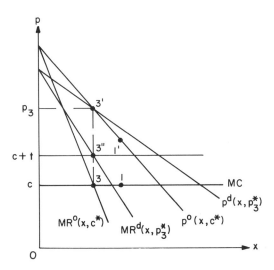

Figure 5.9

tax in place, the domestic exporter maximizes profits by equating the tax-inclusive marginal costs to his perceived marginal revenue at point 3'', and he chooses the optimal price p_3. The optimal tax equals the difference between perceived and true marginal revenue.

This analysis has been for the case of a single domestic exporter. If there are several domestic exporters, of course, the case for an export tax is strengthened: since one firm, by increasing its price, raises the sales of its domestic as well as its foreign rivals, there is an externality that other things equal leads export prices to be too low.

Thus we have now seen that the case for strategic export subsidies is a very fragile one indeed. When competition is Bertrand, an export tax is always optimal; even when competition is Cournot, a tax rather than a subsidy raises welfare, unless the domestic industry is highly concentrated. Thus there would seem to be a presumption toward export taxes rather than export subsidies, except in rare cases.

5.4 Entry with Increasing Returns

Our discussion of export policies in the presence of a domestic oligopoly has so far been restricted to situations in which the number of firms is fixed. It applies therefore to cases in which policies are expected to have no effect on entry and exit decisions of domestic exporters. This, however, is not a very safe assumption. If entry is limited by the size of the market in the presence of increasing returns, then a policy that raises the profits of existing firms may well induce new exporters to enter the industry. Their entry will change the degree of concentration of the industry, the resulting equilibrium, and the desirability of the export subsidy.

This point is readily seen from the formula for welfare changes which we discussed in section 2.7 [equation (2.4)]:

$$dU = dp^*X + p^*dX + \Sigma_i p_i dX_i,$$

where p^* denotes the price paid by foreign buyers, X denotes its volume, and p_i and X_i are prices and quantities of all other goods. If there are n domestic producers and the resulting equilibrium is always symmetrical, then $X = nx$, where x denotes output per firm. Now also assume that every exporting firm has fixed costs of production f and constant marginal costs c, so that its cost function is $f + cx$. (The fixed costs introduce increasing returns to scale, which may be the source of imperfect competition.) Then by treating the number of producers as a continuous variable, the formula implies that

$$dU = dp^*X + (p^* - c)dX - fdn.$$

The first term on the right-hand side represents the terms of trade effect. A policy-induced increase in the export price benefits the country. If it also raises exports, it raises GNP because the export industry prices goods above marginal costs (the other sectors are assumed to be competitive). When new firms enter, however, this production efficiency gain must be weighed against the rise in fixed costs represented by the last term.

It is immediately obvious that the possibility of entry further weakens the case for aggressive export policies while reinforcing that for taxation of exports. We saw that with a fixed number of firms under Cournot conduct, an export subsidy worsens the terms of trade but generates a positive production efficiency effect that outweighs the welfare loss from the deterioration of the terms of trade, provided the number of firms is sufficiently small. Once the possibility of entry is introduced, however, the increase in fixed costs reinforces the terms of trade loss so that an export subsidy is that much less likely to be welfare improving. Conversely, an export tax, which improves the terms of trade but has a negative own-production effect, now produces the additional benefit of encouraging exit and thereby reduces fixed cost.

The case is particularly clear when there is free entry that drives profits to zero. Notice that when a product is only exported, not consumed domestically, the welfare gain that results from its export is simply the profits net of subsidies and taxes earned by the exporter. Namely, the contribution of exports to domestic welfare can be measured by $n\pi + (t - s)X$. Thus the change in welfare that results from an export tax or subsidy may be measured by the sum of its effects on exporter profits and its budgetary impact.

But this means that with free entry a subsidy can never raise welfare because by definition, it costs money and profits are zero (so that profits net of subsidy are negative). When an export subsidy is applied, even under circumstances that may superficially meet the criteria for export subsidy, entry of new firms swallows not only the potential profit gains but the subsidy bill as well, and unambiguously reduces welfare. Under free entry export subsidies can do only harm, whatever their effect on market shares, foreign production, and so on, because they cost the government revenue, which is all that matters (see Horstmann and Markusen 1986).

The optimal policy is, of course, not free trade but an export tax, and the criterion for that tax is simple. It is simply to choose the tax rate that maximizes revenue. The size of this revenue-maximizing tax will depend on specifics of market structure and behavior, but its sign will be unambiguous.

5.5 Resource Constraints

Having raised the possibility of justifying strategic export promotion, we have now identified a series of reasons why it may not be a good idea: competition among domestic firms, uncertainty about oligopolistic conduct, and entry by new firms. However, there is still more to say. Whatever is left of the apparent initial justification for activist export promotion must be qualified further by the fact that imperfectly competitive sectors compete for resources, by the problem of retaliation by foreign governments, and finally by the question of what happens to domestic consumers. We turn in this section to the issue of intersectoral competition for resources.

There are, in principle, two types of intersectoral interactions that need to be considered: among exporting industries and between the group of exporting industries and the rest of the economy. We have dealt to some extent with both via the specification of marginal costs. However, up to this point we have assumed that the marginal production costs of an industry correctly measure resource costs to the economy. This is true only if perfect competition reigns everywhere else: both factor markets and the markets for all other goods must be perfectly competitive. Realistically, however, imperfect competition should be viewed as widespread across the economy. Thus an expansion of any one industry pulls resources from other noncompetitive sectors (or more generally from sectors in which resource allocation is inefficient without policy intervention), and as a result marginal costs of production do not reflect true social marginal costs unless optimal policies are used in these sectors. As in other cases of similar nature a full-fledged analysis requires a full-fledged general equilibrium model. We will, however, continue our approach of concentrating on one particular aspect at a time. For this reason we assume for the rest of this section that all sectors other than those that are explicitly considered are competitive.

The basic insight, which is due to Dixit and Grossman (1986), may be stated simply. To the extent that an imperfectly competitive export industry competes with other imperfectly competitive sectors for resources, export subsidies to that industry will drive up the prices of these resources, acting as an export disincentive elsewhere. Against any strategic gain in the promoted industry, then, must be set strategic disadvantages indirectly imposed on other sectors. It is therefore not enough to show that a favored sector achieves an increase in profits net of subsidy because there may be hidden losses resulting from the indirect effects of the policy.

Specifically, imagine an economy in which there are two oligopolistic sectors that produce for an export market. Industry 1 has sales of X_1, and industry 2 sales of X_2. Rather than describing the demand facing each industry explicitly, we suppose it is possible to define for each a true marginal revenue curve $MR_i(X_i)$, $i = 1, 2$. We also suppose that given the market structure of each industry, we can define a perceived marginal revenue $\widetilde{MR}_i(X_i)$.[9]

---

9. We are implicitly presuming here that the responses of foreign producers in the two industries are independent—for example, subsidizing our exports in industry 1 does not push foreign factors of production into industry 2. This is somewhat awkward, since in our analysis of policy we are presuming precisely this kind of inter-

Now so far in our analysis we have offered a simple rule: subsidize exports if $MR > \widetilde{MR}$; tax them if the reverse is true. This is the correct rule if there are no resource constraints tying the industries together. It ceases to be right, however, if such constraints do exist.

Following Dixit and Grossman (1986), we introduce resource constraints in the following simple way. Each sector is assumed to use only one input: scientists. We choose units so that in each sector it takes one scientist to produce one unit of output. We also assume that there is a fixed supply of scientists, who can be shifted freely between sectors but cannot be employed elsewhere. The wage rate of scientists, w, adjusts so as to clear the market.

The allocation of scientists between the two sectors may now be analyzed. In each sector perceived marginal revenue will be set equal to marginal cost, but marginal cost is the wage rate of a scientist, w, plus any taxes paid minus any subsidy. Thus

$$\widetilde{MR}_i(X_i) = w + t_i - s_i, \qquad i = 1, 2. \tag{5.6}$$

Meanwhile total output is constrained by the limited supply of scientists, $\overline{S}$:

$$X_1 + X_2 = \overline{S}. \tag{5.7}$$

This simple model may be illustrated graphically, as shown in figure 5.10. Industry 1's output is measured from the left, and industry 2's from the right. The length of the figure's base thus represents the supply of scientists. The figure also shows both the true marginal revenue and the perceived marginal revenue curves for each sector. In each case it is assumed (despite the reasons that we have given in earlier sections of this chapter to doubt this result) that $\widetilde{MR} < MR$ so that an economist who has ignored the resource constraint would recommend an export subsidy for each.

In the absence of taxes or subsidies, the equilibrium will be at point 1 in the figure, where the perceived marginal revenues are equal to each other. Obviously, this is unlikely to be the optimal result. Scientists should be allocated so as to equalize true rather than perceived marginal revenue. As the figure is drawn, this requires *less* output from industry 1 and more output from industry 2. In particular, industry 1 should reduce its output to the point where perceived

dependence among domestic industries. However, the basic point of the analysis would not change if these further interdependencies were introduced.

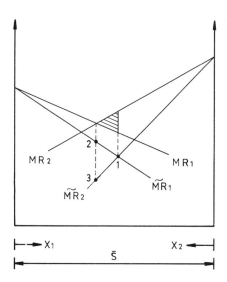

Figure 5.10

marginal revenue is indicated by point 2, whereas industry 2 should increase its output to the point where perceived marginal revenue is indicated by 3.

We can now make several observations. First is that policies based on observations of particular industries in isolation can be wrong-headed. Industry 1 is characterized by an excess of actual over per-ceived marginal revenue and therefore seems to be an appropriate target for subsidy. Yet subsidizing the sector would actually move us away from the optimum and would reduce national welfare.

A second observation is that the gains from even the appropriate policy will be smaller than single-industry analysis might suggest. A naive view might expect that the gains from the optimal expansion of industry 2 are equal to the whole of the excess of actual over perceived MR; in fact, they are only equal to the shaded triangle in figure 5.10, which is much smaller.

A third point is that a variety of tax or subsidy policies can induce the optimal reallocation of resources. All that is necessary is to drive a wedge between the resource cost to sectors 1 and 2 that is equal to the vertical distance between points 2 and 3 in figure 5.10. The wedge, however, equals

$$t_1 - t_2 + s_2 - s_1.$$

Thus there are an infinite number of combinations of the four instruments that will achieve the same result. The policy moral of this observation is that what matters for policy is the net effect of many policy instruments, which cannot be assessed in isolation.

The result changes when the supply of scientific effort is elastic. This may result from entry of college graduates into this field or from changes in hours worked by the existing scientists. In either case their real wage rate influences the available input, and the policies just discussed affect the wage rate. This influence of policies on the supply of scientists needs to be taken into account, for it limits substantially the range of instrument combinations that support an efficient allocation.

5.6 Two-Way Export Policies

Suppose that a country has somehow resolved to its satisfaction all the difficulties we have enumerated in previous sections and is prepared to undertake a strategic export policy. It is still not home free: it must now be concerned with how the governments of other countries will respond.

The interaction of government policies may be modeled as a two-stage game. In the first stage governments choose policy instruments, taking as given other governments' policies. In the second stage private agents make their choices, taking as given the policies established in the first stage. A reasonable consistency requirement that we impose on the outcome of this two-stage game is that governments acting in the first stage take into account the effects of their policies on the second-stage outcome (in the terminology of game theory, the solution is subgame perfect). The results of policies in this type of an environment can be quite different from an environment in which other governments maintain fixed policies. The importance of this point is demonstrated in the remainder of this section by the interactions of two governments and two firms.

We consider a special case of the model we set out in section 5.2. As before, a domestic and a foreign firm export to a third market. To focus the issue more clearly, we now add the assumption that the two firms are *symmetric*—that is, they face the same marginal costs of production, and if their products are imperfect substitutes, they face symmetrical demand functions. As before, since there are no domestic consumers, the objective of each government is to maximize profits net of taxes and subsidies.

First we consider the case in which the firms compete in Cournot fashion. Their reaction curves in the absence of intervention are shown as RR and R^*R^* in figure 5.11. Since the two firms are symmetrical, the reaction curves are also symmetrical, and they intersect on the 45° line, implying equal equilibrium sales.

From the arguments presented in section 5.2, however, we can immediately see that point 1 is not an equilibrium in the two-stage game because each government has an incentive to provide an export subsidy, thereby shifting the second-stage outcome in its favor. For example, at point 1 home profits are represented by the isoprofit curve π_1, which is above R^*R^* to the right of 1. An export subsidy to the home-country firm shifts its reaction curve to the right, so that in the absense of changes in the foreign government's policy the second-stage outcome can be shifted to 1', which provides a higher net of subsidy profit level to the home firm. Clearly, a similar argument applies to the foreign country. Hence both governments have an incentive to subsidize exports (see Brander and Spencer 1985). At a symmetrical equilibrium of the two-stage game, both will end up with the same subsidy rate. This rate brings about equilibrium reaction curves such as R_2R_2 and $R_2^*R_2^*$, which also intersect on the 45° line. The equilibrium point 2 is characterized by tangency of a

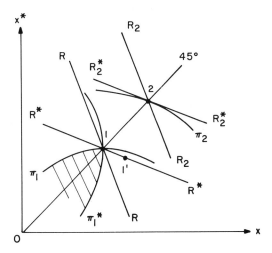

Figure 5.11

subsidy-exclusive profit curve π_2 and the foreign reaction curve (by symmetry, at this point a foreign isoprofit curve is tangent to the domestic firm's reaction curve). This tangency condition ensures that further increases in the subsidy do not raise profits net of subsidy.

It is evident from the figure that both countries have lower profits (and therefore welfare) at point 2. Hence competitive subsidization of exports leads to an inferior outcome for both. If the governments can agree to abstain from export promotion, both will be better off. Each government, however, has an incentive to promote exports whatever the other does, leading to a Prisoner's Dilemma type of situation.

If full cooperation could be achieved, the governments would in fact end up taxing rather than subsidizing their exports. The shaded area in figure 5.11 indicates outcomes that are preferred by both to free trade (and free trade is preferred to export subsidies). By taxing exports at a common rate, the governments could ensure outcomes on the 45° line in the shaded area. This way they share equally in the benefits of a joint trade policy. The reason that export taxes are the suitable instruments is, of course, that under free trade the firms act as a noncooperative duopoly. Consequently they jointly produce more than a monopolist would do in similar circumstances. Thus their jointly optimal strategy is to produce the monopoly output level, exploiting to a maximum the third market.

The case illustrated in figure 5.11 has attracted wide interest among international economists and political scientists because it corresponds nicely to the preconceptions of many noneconomists, who like to think of international trade competition as being like an arms race. In this example aggressive unilateral export promotion is in each country's interest, yet it is in their joint interest to exercise restraint. Thus an agreement to limit government intervention serves the same function here that an arms limitation treaty serves in military competition.

As we have repeatedly stressed in this chapter, the case for unilateral gains from export promotion is actually a very questionable one. The presumption is that even taking foreign policies as given, the optimal policy in an imperfectly competitive export sector is probably a tax rather than a subsidy. This changes the nature of the interaction between governments, making the problem more like that of pollution control or funding of basic research than that of an arms race.

To see this, consider the case we examined in section 5.3 where firms compete in prices instead of quantities. Figure 5.12 illustrates the interaction between two firms producing imperfect substitutes. The reaction curves RR and R^*R^* describe the outcome in the absence of government intervention. Absent government action, the equilibrium is at point 1, which is on the 45° line as a result of our symmetry assumptions. The isoprofit curves π_1 and π_1^* show the incentive to intervene. If the domestic government believes that the foreign government will not intervene, it can increase its firm's net of tax profits by *taxing* exports. As we explained in section 5.3, taxation of exports leads the domestic firm to respond with a higher price for every foreign price. Hence its reaction curve shifts to the right, and in the absence of the foreign government's response the equilibrium point shifts to the right on the foreign firm's reaction curve. For sufficiently small tax rates, the new equilibrium point is above the π_1 isoprofit curve, implying higher net of tax profits for the home country and therefore higher welfare. The same incentive exists in the foreign country. So point 1 is not an equilibrium in the two-stage game. The equilibrium of the two-stage game is, instead, at a point like 2, where the tax-inclusive reaction curves R_2R_2 and $R_2^*R_2^*$ intersect and the net of taxes isoprofit curve π_2 is tangent to the foreign reaction curve. Naturally, in this case the foreign net of taxes isoprofit curve is also tangent to the home reaction curve at 2.

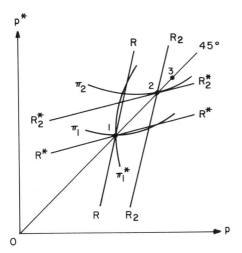

Figure 5.12

Two important points emerge from a comparison of this equilibrium with the outcome in the Cournot case. First, here the two-stage game brings about trade taxes rather than subsidies. This results from the fact that prices are strategic complements, whereas quantities in the Cournot game are strategic substitutes. Second, here competitive trade policy does not generate a Prisoner's Dilemma type of situation because point 2 is preferred to 1 by both parties. Hence the policy-induced equilibrium is preferred to free trade. This too stems from the fact that prices are strategic complements, which calls for restricting trade. Since in free trade firms charge prices that are too low relative to joint profit maximization—and therefore they produce too much relative to joint profit maximization—the resulting policy-induced equilibrium, which restricts exports, brings about higher joint profits. Given the symmetrical structure of exports, the higher joint profits are equally shared.

Now point 2 is still not the optimum. To see this, we note that the isoprofit curves at 2 are tangent to the reaction curves, (i.e., have different slopes), whereas at an optimum (which must be on the contract curve) they must be tangent to each other. Thus the optimum must be at a point like 3. In other words, it is in the joint interest of the countries to do *more*, not less, trade intervention—to charge higher export taxes. The problem is therefore the reverse of that illustrated in figure 5.11. Whereas our first example looked like an arms race, where agreement was needed to get everyone to do less, our second (and more probable) case looks like the problem of funding world basic research, where agreement is needed to get everyone to do more.

5.7 Consumption Effects

Our analysis of export policies has so far disregarded consumption effects in the exporting country. This abstraction helped to underline the role of export policies in raising GNP and their relationship to conduct and market structure. It is, however, well known that domestic use of exportables introduces additional considerations that relate to the efficient servicing of domestic markets. Thus export policies that maximize the value of output are not optimal unless domestic use of exportables is also at the optimal level. For this reason we discuss in this section the necessary modifications in our policy conclusions when exportables are also used at home.

In the presence of domestic consumption our general formula for welfare changes (2.4) implies that

$$dU = dpX_f + (p_C - c)dX_d + (p - c)dX_f,$$

where p denotes the price charged in export markets, p_C denotes the price payed by domestic consumers (users), X_f represents exports, X_d represents domestic consumption of exportables (domestic use), and c is marginal costs. This derivation assumes that in all other industries domestic price equals marginal cost and that c represents true marginal costs in terms of forgone income in other sectors. This is of course the standard formula in which the first term represents the terms of trade effect, the second represents the consumption wedge effect, and the third represents the production efficiency effect.

For current purposes we assume that only domestic firms serve the domestic market; that is, it is prohibitively costly for foreign firms to export to the domestic market (we discuss cross-market penetration in chapter 7). For this reason X_d is part of domestic production. In addition we restrict the discussion to the case of a homogeneous exportable. It is, however, not difficult to see how to interpret the results for an industry that produces a fixed number of imperfectly substitutable commodities, as long as everything is symmetrical.

To bring out as clearly as possible the relationship between the current analysis and the results from previous sections, we rewrite the formula for welfare changes in the following way:

$$dU = [d(pX_f) - cdX_f] + (p_C - c)dX_d. \tag{5.11}$$

In this representation the first term applies to exports, and the second applies to domestic use. A characterization of the first-best policy is now straightforward. Exports are at their optimal level when the *true* marginal revenue equals marginal costs, and domestic use is at its optimal level when the domestic price equals marginal costs. Naturally, at this allocation the domestic users' price also equals true marginal revenue from exports. These relationships represent the correct shadow pricing. There are two ways in which domestic consumption can be satisfied: by producing more or by exporting less. The optimality conditions ensure that both alternatives are equally costly.

To identify policies that support the optimal allocation, we need to specify conduct and market structure. We illustrate a suitable procedure for the case of Cournot conduct and a fixed number of firms. Consider the case in which the price of exports depends on X_f and foreign sales; that is, $p = p[X_f + \rho^*(X_f)]$, where $\rho^*(\cdot)$ represents the foreign reaction function. Then optimal exports have to satisfy (5.3b), which expresses equality of true marginal revenue with marginal costs. This can be achieved by a net export subsidy described in (5.4) (the net export subsidy may be negative, implying taxation of exports). Now observe that in the absence of domestic use of exportables, taxation or subsidization of exports was equivalent to taxation or subsidization of production. It is, however, clear from the foregoing discussion that in the presence of domestic use export should be targeted rather than production.

Next, consider a policy that attains the optimal level of domestic consumption. A given number n of domestic firms competes for domestic sales. Each firm chooses domestic sales so as to equate perceived marginal revenue to marginal costs. Let $p_C(X_d)$ be the inverse demand function of domestic users, as perceived by domestic producers of exportables (we disregard income effects). Then if s_d denotes the subsidy on domestic sales, a typical domestic producer will choose domestic sales so as to equate perceived marginal revenue with net of subsidy marginal production costs:

$$p_C(X_d) + \frac{p'_C(X_d)X_d}{n} = c(X_d + X_f) - s_d. \tag{5.12a}$$

It is clear from this formula (in which we allow marginal costs to depend on total output) that when optimal exports are attained by means of the suitable export tax, optimal domestic consumption is attained by a domestic sales subsidy that equals $-p'_C(X_d)X_d/n$, where X_d equals the optimal consumption level. Thus the subsidy brings about a reduction of the domestic price to the level of marginal production costs. In other words, the subsidy offsets the oligopolists' markup. It is now easy to see that the optimal consumption and export taxes can be replaced by an output subsidy supplemented with an export tax. This can be done as follows. Let the output subsidy equal the optimal consumption subsidy s_d. Then, if s_f represents the optimal net export subsidy in the presence of the consumption tax, let the export subsidy in the absence of the consumption tax be $s_f - s_d$ (in addition to the output subsidy). In this case the two schemes generate precisely the same incentives to export and sell in the domestic market, thereby bringing about an identical allocation of resources. However, since the consumption subsidy is necessarily positive, under the latter scheme exports are taxed whether they are taxed or subsidized under the former scheme.

References

Brander, James A., and Spencer, Barbara J. (1985). "Export subsidies and market share rivalry." *Journal of International Economics* 18: 83–100.

Carmichael, Calum (1987). "The control of export credit subsidies and its welfare consequences." *Journal of International Economics* 23: 1–19.

Dixit, Avinash K. (1984). "International trade policy for oligopolistic industries." *Economic Journal* (supplement) 16.

Dixit, Avinash K., and Grossman, Gene M. (1986). "Targeted export promotion with several oligopolistic industries." *Journal of International Economics* 21: 233–250.

Eaton, Jonathan, and Grossman, Gene M. (1986). "Optimal trade and industrial policy under oligopoly." *Quarterly Journal of Economics* 101: 383–406.

Gruenspecht, Howard K. (1988). "Export subsidies for differentiated products." *Journal of International Economics* 24: 331–344.

Horstmann, Ignatius, and Markusen, James R. (1986). "Up the average cost curve: Inefficient entry and the new protectionism." *Journal of International Economics* 20: 225–247.

Krishna, Kala, and Thursby, Marie (1988). "Optimal policies with strategic distortions." NBER Working Paper No. 2527.

Tirole, Jean (1988). *The Theory of Industrial Organization*. Cambridge, MA: The MIT Press.

6   Strategic Import Policy

In the past three chapters we have followed a strategy of isolating different aspects of market power in trade. Thus in chapter 3 an imperfectly competitive domestic industry faced a perfectly competitive supply of goods from abroad; in chaper 4 an imperfectly competitive foreign industry sold into a domestic market characterized either by an absence of domestic production or by price-taking firms. In chapter 5 we focused on the problem of strategic competition by considering industries that compete in a third market, leaving aside the question of how interventionist trade policies affect domestic consumers.

In reality, of course, such clean distinctions are rare. An industry that is imperfectly competitive at home will usually be so abroad as well, and vice versa; a good that is exported will usually be consumed domestically as well (and often imported in different varieties, since intraindustry trade is common in imperfectly competitive industries). The normal context of trade policy is therefore one in which both domestic and foreign firms have market power and in which policy must concern itself with consumer as well as producer surplus.

In this chapter we turn to the consideration of the effects of trade policy in a market in which foreign and domestic firms with market power compete for the domestic market. Not surprisingly, this market structure, which combines many feaures from previous chapters, also raises a number of the previous issues. In addition it gives rise to some new issues as well.

6.1 Tariffs: The Cournot Case

In chapter 4 we showed that under some circumstances an import tariff levied on imperfectly competitive foreign exporters will be partially absorbed by the foreigners and thus raise domestic welfare. We begin this chapter's analysis by considering the same policy in the case where there is an imperfectly competitive domestic industry as well. The question is whether a tariff is more or less likely to benefit the importing country than in the one-sided case. When competition is Cournot in form, the answer is that a tariff is considerably more likely to be beneficial.

We show this by demonstrating three ways in which the criterion for domestic gains from a tariff is weaker under Cournot competition than in the one-sided case. First, even when the market demand curve is such that a foreign monopolist would raise her price more than the tariff, the presence of a single domestic competitor shifts the perceived demand curve in a way that makes absorption of the tariff more likely. Second, a tariff induces an increase in domestic output that further limits price increases, making it still more likely that a tariff will be partially absorbed. Finally, a tariff will shift profits from foreign to domestic producers, making it still more likely that domestic welfare will increase.

Consider, then, an industry where there are two producers of the same good: a domestic firm that produces for its home market, and a foreign firm that exports into that market. Let x denote the domestic firm's output, m the level of imports supplied by the foreign firm, and $z = x + m$ the total market supply. We can represent domestic demand by an inverse demand function $p = p(z)$. We also suppose that each firm has constant marginal cost: c for the domestic firm and c^* for the foreign firm.

Let us now suppose that each firm chooses deliveries to the domestic market, taking the other firm's deliveries as given. In figure 6.1 the curve RR represents the domestic firm's reaction curve, whereas $R_1^* R_1^*$ represents the foreign firm's reaction curve in the absence of a tariff. The free trade equilibrium is therefore at point 1.

If the domestic government imposes a specific tariff, this will in effect raise the foreign firm's marginal cost, shifting its reaction curve bck to $R_2^* R_2^*$.[1] Home output rises from x_1 to x_2, while the level of imports falls from m_1 to m_2. The price in the domestic market rises,

---

1. A similar analysis applies to an ad valorem tariff; it shifts the reaction curve to the

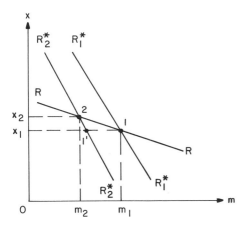

Figure 6.1

and therefore so does the tariff-inclusive price of imports. However, the price may rise either more or less than the tariff, so that the import price net of tariffs may either rise or fall.

The welfare effects of the tariff reflect several components; two cases are illustrated in figures 6.2 and 6.3. In figure 6.2 we show the case where the import price rises by more than the amount of the tariff, so that $p_2 - t > p_1$. In figure 6.3 we show the case where the price rises by less than the tariff, so that $p_2 - t < p_1$.

Consider the case in figure 6.2 first. The tariff has three effects on Home welfare: it reduces consumer surplus, it increases producer surplus, and it generates government revenue. The loss in consumer surplus is the whole area under the demand curve lost when the price increase from p_1 to p_2; in the figure it is represented by the sum of the labeled areas $a + b + c + d + e$. The increase in producer surplus is the sum of the increased price of what the domestic firms would have sold under free trade, plus the difference between price and marginal cost multiplied by the increase in output as a result of the tariff. The whole increase in producer surplus is therefore $a + b + f$. Finally, the government collects revenue equal to the post-

---

left. We have seen in chapter 4, however, that specific and ad valorem tariffs are not equivalent from a welfare point of view when the foreign suppliers are not competitive. This feature applies here as well. To avoid too much repetition, however, we discuss in this chapter specific tariffs only.

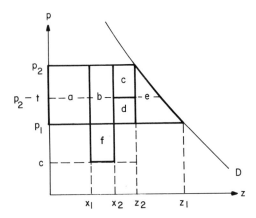

Figure 6.2

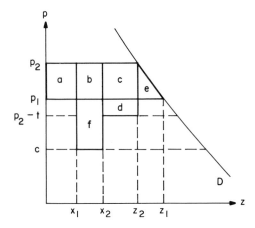

Figure 6.3

tariff level of imports multiplied by the tariff rate, or area c. Netting out offsetting areas, we end up with the effects of areas e, f, and d. The loss items are e, which represents a consumption distortion loss, and d, which represents a terms of trade loss. The benefit is f, which represents a production efficiency gain. That is, the strategic role of trade policy, which we examined in the previous chapter in the competition for the export market, reappears here in the effects of a tariff on competition in the domestic market.

For a small tariff, triangles become insignificant so that the area e can be neglected. This point can also be seen by applying (2.5) to obtain

$$dU = - mdp^* + (p - c)dx,$$

where the first term, the terms of trade term, corresponds to the area d, and the second term, the production efficiency term, corrresponds to the area f. The net effect of a small tariff, then, is in this case to produce a terms of trade loss and a production efficiency gain.

The terms of trade, however, need not be worsened by a tariff. Figure 6.3 shows the opposite case, where the price rises by less than the tariff. Here the consumer loss is $a + b + c + e$, while the producer gain is $a + b + f$. Government revenue is $c + d$. The net effect on welfare, then, is shown by e, d, and f. The only loss item is e, the consumption distortion loss. Part of the government revenue, the area d, represents a terms of trade gain. And the production efficiency gain f represents a further source of gain. In the case of a small tariff the consumption distortion becomes negligible, so the overall effect must be a national gain in welfare.

We see, then, that a tariff can produce a gain for the protecting country. However, we already saw this possibility in chapter 4. The natural question is whether the presence of an imperfectly competitive domestic industry raises or lowers the likelihood of this gain. What we can show is that *for a given demand curve*, a small tariff is more likely to raise welfare if there is an imperfectly competitive domestic industry.

Recall that a specific tariff imposed on a foreign monopolist will raise the import price by less than the tariff, and thus generate a terms of trade gain, if marginal revenue is steeper than the demand curve itself. The slope of the demand curve is $p'(z)$, and revenue for a monopolist is $p(z)z$. So marginal revenue is $p(z) + zp'(z)$ and the slope of marginal revenue is $zp''(z) + 2p'(z)$. If $p''(z) \leq 0$, then marginal revenue will always be steeper than demand, which includes the case of linear demand. If $p''(z) > 0$, however, marginal revenue *may* (though it need not) be flatter than demand, in which case a specific tariff will raise prices by more than the tariff. As it turns out, the case of constant elasticity demand is one in which the price rises by more than the tariff.

Now suppose that the demand curve is the same as in the case of a foreign monopolist, but this time there is also a domestic competitor. What we can show is that for any demand curve for which the price would have risen less than the tariff with a foreign monopolist, it will still rise less in the case of a duopoly. But for some demand curves under which the price would have risen by more than the tariff for a monopolist, it will rise less for a duopolist. In other words, a terms of trade gain is definitely more likely under duopoly.

To see this, we artificially break the consequences of the tariff into two parts. First, we ask what would happen if the output of the domestic firm did not change. This amounts to asking what the *perceived* demand curve of the foreign firm under the Cournot assumption looks like; it is the price change that would result if in figure 6.1 we moved only from point 1 to 1', not to point 2. We then ask what the secondary consequences of the induced rise in output, and the consequent move from 1' to 2, are for the terms of trade.

Consider, then, the hypothetical movement from 1 to 1'. If domestic output x is held constant, the slope of the demand curve perceived by the foreign firm is the same as that of the market demand, $p'(z)$. However, the foreign firm's revenue is only part of total sales in the market $mp(z)$, where $m < z$. So the marginal revenue curve facing the foreign firm is $mp'(z) + p(z)$, and the slope of that curve is $mp''(z) + 2p'(z)$, compared with $zp''(z) + 2p'(z)$ in the monopoly case.

Since $m < z$, the slope of the marginal revenue curve is flatter than in the monopoly case if $p''(z) < 0$, steeper if $p''(z) > 0$. However, if $p''(z) < 0$, the marginal revenue curve is in either case steeper than the demand curve, implying that a tariff improves the terms of trade. If $p''(z) > 0$, the marginal revenue curve may be flatter than the demand curve; however, this is less likely now than in the monopoly case. Thus when we move from 1 to 1' in figure 6.1, any demand curve for which the terms of trade improve in the monopoly case will also involve an improvement in the terms of trade in the duopoly case, and some demand curves that would have implied worse terms of trade now imply better terms of trade.

Furthermore this is not the whole story, because we still have to take into account the move from 1' to 2. This move necessarily involves a fall in the price. To see this, note that the marginal revenue perceived by the foreign firm must be equal to $c^* + t$ at all points along $R_2^* R_2^*$. However, if the price were to remain unchanged, so would the slope of the demand curve $p'(z)$, and therefore the marginal revenue $p(z) + mp'(z)$ would have risen. Therefore p must have fallen. But this fall in price is added to the initial change in price, which we have seen is already more likely to involve partial absorption of the tariff than in the monopoly case.

We have therefore arrived at the following result: *when there is a domestic competitor to a foreign monopolist, and the firms play Cournot, it is more likely that a specific tariff will improve the terms of trade than if there were no domestic firm.*

Nor is this the end of the story. Even if a tariff fails to improve the terms of trade, it may still improve welfare through the production efficiency gain, as we noted in figures 6.2 and 6.3. We can therefore see that it is quite likely that a tariff will raise welfare in this case— this may not quite be a presumption, but it looks quite probable.

6.2 Tariffs: The Bertrand Case

It is at least as reasonable to assume that firms compete in prices as to assume that they compete in quantities. If competition takes place in prices, however, the logic that we used to construct a near presumption that tariffs improve welfare needs to be qualified. Now the presence of a domestic competitor is not necessarily a force making tariffs more likely to be beneficial.

Suppose that, as before, a domestic and a foreign firm are producing goods that are imperfect substitutes. We know that under Bertrand competition each firm's behavior may be normally characterized by an upward-sloping reaction function in price space—that is, the higher the other firm's price, the higher the price our firm will charge. Typical reaction functions are shown in figure 6.4, with RR representing the reactions of the domestic firm and $R_1^* R_1^*$ the foreign firm's behavior in the absence of a tariff. Equilibrium is at point 1.

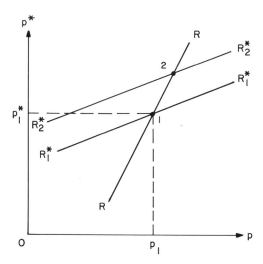

Figure 6.4

A specific tariff here, as always, is like an increase in the foreign firm's marginal cost. This shifts the reaction curve out, to $R_2^* R_2^*$, raising the prices of both firms, as the new equilibrium is at point 2.

The difference from the Cournot case is immediately apparent. The strategic effect of the tariff—that is, its effect in changing the game played by the firms—weakens instead of reinforcing the willingness of the foreign firm to absorb the tariff. The rise in the price of the domestic good encourages a second-round rise in the price of the foreign good, which in turn encourages a further rise in the price of the domestic good, and so on. It is therefore less likely that the foreign firm will absorb part of the tariff than if domestic firms did not respond. It is even possible that the responses of domestic firms will actually raise the profits of the foreign firm so that the tariff is a benefit for the foreigners rather than a cost.

How much difference does this make? It is important to recognize that figure 6.4 and figure 6.1 are in different spaces—it is invalid to simply claim that domestic competition reinforces the incentives for tariff absorption in one case while reducing them in the other. Notice that if we compare the qualitative effects on the firms in the two cases, they are similar: in either case the price and output of the domestic firm rise, while the price of the foreign firm must rise and its output fall.

6.3 Import Quotas

In chapters 3 and 4 we saw that import quotas, which in competitive models are equivalent in their effects to tariffs (except possibly for the revenue consequences), may be quite different in their effect when competition is imperfect. This remains the case in the present analysis, although now the results depend qualitatively as well as quantitatively on the form taken by competition.

Consider first the case of Cournot competition. The effect of an import quota is to limit the foreign firm's deliveries to the amount of the quota. The domestic firm's reaction curve, however, was based precisely on taking the foreign firm's deliveries as given. Thus the quota simply shifts the equilibrium down the home reaction curve, which is the same as what happens with a tariff.

The difference comes in the disposition of revenues. As in the case of a foreign monopolist facing a quota, which we analyzed in chapter 4, the foreign firm can always choose in this case to deliver slightly less than the quota so that the quota rents accrue entirely as foreign profits rather than as income to license-holders. Thus in this case the quota cannot be equivalent to a tariff, even if the quota is auctioned off; the quota shows up as a worsening of the terms of trade. Notice that this clearly implies that from a national point of view quotas are worse than tariffs.[2]

The Bertrand case, by contrast, is one in which quotas have dramatically different effects from tariffs. This case was first analyzed by Krishna (1985), who showed that seemingly simple conditions can give rise to remarkably complex behavior. We therefore turn to the surprisingly strange story of the effects of an import quota on Bertrand competition between domestic and foreign firms.

It will be useful to begin by focusing on what may appear to be a special case. This is the case that we used in the analysis of cartels in chapters 3 and 4 where we imposed an import quota that restricts imports *not to exceed their free trade level*. In a competitive world such a quota would not be binding at all. As we know, however, in an imperfectly competitive world the quota may indeed matter. Furthermore, once we understand this case, it will turn out to be straightforward to understand many other cases as well.

---

2. See also Hwang and Mai (1988) for a comparison of tariffs and quotas for a duopoly with conjectural variations. They, however, disregard the distributional effect of quota rents.

Suppose, then, that we start from the free trade equilibrium shown as point 1 in figure 6.4 and impose a quota that limits imports not to exceed that level. To analyze the implications of this, we look first at the incentives provided to the domestic firm, holding the foreign firm's price unchanged at p_1^*.

In figure 6.5, D represents the demand curve that the home firm perceives itself as facing under free trade. This demand curve is drawn under the assumption of a constant price for the foreign good. When a quota is binding, however, as we noted in chapter 3, a demand for foreign goods that exceeds the quota will be reflected in a premium on imports, collected as a rent by holders of import licenses. It seems reasonable here to suppose, as in earlier models, that the home firm takes this effect into account—that is, that it is a Bertrand player with respect to the foreign firm's quoted price but is aware that it can affect the price to domestic consumers.

This implies that once the quota is imposed, the perceived demand curve for prices above the free trade level is higher and steeper than under free trade, a result illustrated by D' in figure 6.5.

Now consider the effect on marginal revenue. In figure 6.5 we show the relevant marginal revenue curve under the quota, still holding the foreign firm's price at its free trade level. For output just below the free trade level x_1, the steeper demand curve implies a lower marginal revenue MR' than the flatter curve MR to the right of x_1. The former corresponds to D', and the latter corresponds to D. Hence there is now a discontinuity in marginal revenue. The

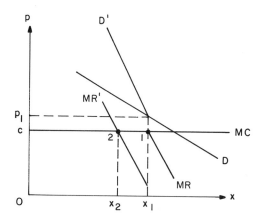

Figure 6.5

original intersection between marginal cost and revenue was at point 1. The new intersection at point 2 yields unambiguously higher profits, since as output is reduced from x_1 to x_2 the reduction in revenue is always less than the reduction in cost. Thus, if the foreign firm's price were at its free trade level, the home firm would always choose to move to a higher price.

What if the foreign firm were to change its price? If it were to charge a *lower* price, the decision of the home firm would not be affected: the home firm could always get to point 2, though the profitability of cutting prices to sally out from behind the import quota would become even less attractive than at the free trade price p_1^*. However, if the foreign firm were to raise its price the result might be to change the home firm's behavior. Figure 6.6 shows the situation with a somewhat higher p^*. The higher foreign price raises the level of p at which the quota becomes binding and raises the demand curve at those prices at which the quota is not binding. The result is therefore to create a second local profit maximum, at point 3.

Which of these local maxima, 2 or 3, is the global maximum? The answer depends on how high p^* is set. For p^* only slightly above its free trade level, it is more profitable for the domestic firm to retreat behind the quota, raising its price to p_2. However, the higher p^* gets, the more attractive point 3 becomes because the shaded area with vertex 3 becomes larger and the shaded area with vertex 2 becomes smaller. At some sufficiently high p^* the home firm will abruptly shift from the "timid" strategy of charging p_2 and accepting the

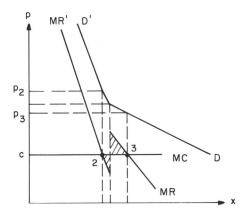

Figure 6.6

protection of the import quota to the "aggressive" strategy of charging p_3, a price that drives imports below the quota level.

This implies that under a quota the reaction curve of the home firm RR is altered from the simple upward-sloping schedule we have assumed for tariff analysis to a discontinuous curve of the kind shown in figure 6.7. For foreign price less than the free trade level and up to some point above, say, p_A^*, the domestic firm raises its price to the "timid" level p_T. When p^* gets high enough, however, the firm emerges from behind the quota, charging the "aggressive" price p_A. Any further increase in p^* will be matched by domestic price increases along the original free trade reaction curve.

Now let's turn to the foreign firm. Its reaction curve will also be shifted by the presence of a quota. There is never any point in the foreign firm's charging a price lower than that which will lead to the complete filling of the import quota, since it cannot sell more than the quota anyway and may as well attempt to capture all of the quota rents. Suppose, then, that we imagine raising the home firm's price gradually above the free trade level. What the foreign firm will do in the presence of a quota is raise its own price enough to just match import demand to the quota. This involves a *greater* rise in p^* than would be the case under free trade. So as we move up from point 1 in figure 6.4, the foreign reaction curve is now steeper. (At lower prices the reaction curve is unchanged.) The resulting foreign reaction curve is as shown in figure 6.7.

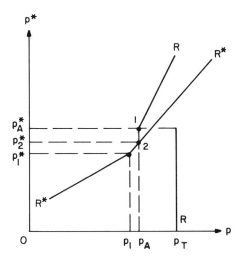

Figure 6.7

This figure embodies one more key result. If the home firm charges the timid price p_T, the foreign firm will charge the maximum price at which the quota is binding. But at this price, the home firm will certainly find charging the aggressive price more profitable. To see this directly, consider figure 6.8. Here the demand curve facing the home firm is shown with the "kink" occurring precisely at p_T, as would be the case if the foreign firm raised its price to appropriate the quota premium. Correspondingly, the marginal revenue curve just touches the marginal cost curve at x_T. It is immediately clear that by reducing its price and increasing its sales to x_A, the domestic firm unambiguously increases its profits: marginal revenue exceeds marginal cost all the way, and the shaded area represents the gain from the aggressive strategy.

But this tells us that the postquota foreign reaction curve *never intersects the home reaction curve. R*R** passes through the "hole" in *RR*!

Obviously, we have a problem. If the foreign firm believes that the home firm will choose a timid strategy, it sets its own price so high that the home firm becomes aggressive. If the foreign firm thinks the home firm will be aggressive, it sets a price low enough that the home firm will, instead, be timid. No straightforward equilibrium exists.

The kind of equilibrium that does exist, as Krishna (1985) pointed out, is a *mixed strategy equilibrium* in which the home firm chooses

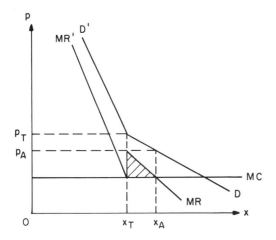

Figure 6.8

prices randomly. Specifically, we can find an equilibrium as follows: the foreign firm sets its price at the level p_A^* in figure 6.7, which is the level that leaves the home firm indifferent between being timid, and retreating behind the quota, or being aggressive, and sallying out into open competition. For its part, the home firm must randomly choose which of these strategies to follow, with the probabilities set so as to make the foreign firm willing to charge p_A^*.

Under what conditions will the foreign firm be willing to charge p_A^*? Consider the effects of an increase in p^* on the foreign firm's profits. If the home firm is following the timid strategy so that the import quota is binding, the effect will be to raise the price received by the foreign firm without reducing sales, that is, to appropriate some of the quota rents. Thus in the timid state $\partial \pi^*/\partial p^* = \overline{m}$, where $\overline{m}$ is the quota level of imports and π^* denotes profits. In the aggressive state, on the other hand, a higher p^* will lower sales as well as raise the price so that the normal marginal revenue calculation applies: $\partial \pi^*/\partial p^* = m_A + (p_A^* - c^*)(\partial m/\partial p^*)$. We note that p_A^* is above p_2^* and that $\partial \pi^*/\partial p^* = 0$ at point 2 (the foreign firm is on its reaction curve). Hence $\partial \pi^*/\partial p^* < 0$ at point 1 in the aggressive case.

To provide the foreign firm with the incentive to charge p_A^*, the expected gains from a change in p^* must be zero. Thus the home firm must charge p_A with a probability λ, and p_T with a probability $1 - \lambda$, so that

$$\lambda \overline{m} + (1 - \lambda)\left[m_A + (p_A^* - c^*)\left(\frac{\partial m}{\partial p^*}\right)\right] = 0,$$

where $\partial m/\partial p^*$ is evaluated at point 1.

The equilibrium, then, is a random one in which the foreign firm always charges p_A^*, but the home firm charges p_A with a probability λ and p_T with a probability $1 - \lambda$. There are a number of interesting points to notice about this equilibrium, which are surprising from the point of view of our normal ideas about what protection does.

First, p_A^* is above the free trade foreign price, as are both p_A and p_T. Thus the quota leads to an unambiguous increase in the prices of both the domestic and foreign firms, even net of the quota rents. In the timid case the price to domestic consumers will be higher than p_A^* because of the premium charged by license-holders.

Although the quota thus has an effect on prices in both states of the world, it need not be filled; in the aggressive case the foreign firms end up selling less than the permitted amount. Nevertheless, prices in this state are higher because of the quota's presence.

When the quota *is* binding, the foreign firm's price is not high enough to fully appropriate the quota rents. This is in contrast both to the case of a foreign monopoly and to the case of Cournot competition.

The quota raises profits of the foreign firm and the expected profits of the domestic firm. This is immediately apparent for the domestic firm, since the price of competing imports is unambiguously higher. To see that it is true for the foreign firm, we can use the following approach. Suppose that the foreign firm were simply to charge its free trade price p_f^*. Then since p_A and p_T are both above p_1, the foreign firm would find itself filling the quota in both states—that is, selling the same amount at the same price as under free trade. So it can guarantee itself at least its free trade level of profitability. Since it then chooses to charge a different price, it must be because it is more profitable. So the foreign firm also earns more profits under the quota than under free trade. As Krishna's paper notes, the import quota is a "facilitating device" that enables the firms to behave in a de facto more collusive manner, benefiting both at consumers' expense.

These are remarkable results. The problem is, of course, that we require the domestic firm to engage in random pricing; otherwise, there is no equilibrium. The practical interpretation of this strategy is, however, not clear.

References

Krishna, Kala (1985). "Trade restrictions as facilitating practices." NBER Working Paper No. 1546. Forthcoming in *Journal of International Economics*.

Hwang, Hong, and Mai, Chao-cheng (1988). "On the equivalence of tariffs and quotas under duopoly: A conjectural variation approach." *Journal of International Economics* 24: 373–380.

Intraindustry Trade

One of the key empirical reasons for emphasizing the role of increasing returns and imperfect competition in the world economy is the apparent prevalence of intraindustry trade. Intraindustry trade may be defined as the two-way exchange of goods in which neither country seems to have a comparative cost advantage. It is a phenomenon that first drew attention during the rapid expansion of trade in manufactured goods that followed the creation of the European Common Market; it now constitutes a significant fraction of the trade of industrial countries, especially between those at similar levels of economic development (see Helpman 1987).

The theoretical literature on intraindustry trade has advanced two quite different possible explanations of the phenomenon. The more popular explanation sees intraindustry trade as the result of the interaction between product differentiation and economies of scale. According to this view, each industry contains a large number of potential differentiated products that consumers regard as imperfect substitutes. Because of economies of scale, however, an individual country can produce only a limited range of products. Given the opportunity to trade, countries will specialize in the production of different ranges, and they will trade in order to satisfy the taste of consumers for variety, or the difference in tastes among consumers, or the demand for a spectrum of differentiated inputs. This standard explanation of intraindustry trade has been elaborated in an extensive literature. We have elsewhere surveyed and synthesized this literature (Helpman and Krugman 1985).

An alternative, more exotic explanation of intraindustry trade was first proposed by Brander (1981) and elaborated by Brander and Krugman (1983). In this view intraindustry trade represents literal two-way trade in identical products. The driving force behind the trade is price discrimination. Firms segment their markets, restricting deliveries to the domestic market in order to keep the price high while selling more aggressively abroad. The result is "reciprocal dumping," in which the willingness of firms to accept a lower markup on exports than on domestic sales gives rise to trade despite the absence of comparative cost differences.

Given the apparent importance of intraindustry trade and the popularity of the basic intraindustry trade models, it is natural to ask what the prevalence of intraindustry trade implies for trade policy. Is it in the national interest to impose tariffs against foreign goods that compete with domestic goods in intraindustry trade?

This chapter begins with a brief presentation of a basic model of a monopolistically competitive equilibrium in a closed economy; this model serves as a building block through the rest of the chapter. We then examine in turn several potential arguments for protection. First is the possibility of using a tariff to improve the terms of trade—an argument that is very much like the traditional optimal tariff argument described in chapter 2 but that has some new twists in the intraindustry case. We highlight the difference from the traditional argument by building a slightly different model in which a tariff cannot alter the terms of trade—yet a case for protection still emerges because protection can increase production efficiency and bring about a beneficial change in variety choice.

We then turn to a more surprising possibility: in the presence of intraindustry trade a tariff may actually lower domestic prices of the protected industry. As we show, this is true in both the differentiated-products model and the segmented-market model of intraindustry trade.

7.1 A Basic Monopolistic Competition Model[1]

We imagine an economy that is able to produce a large number of products, all of which enter symmetrically into demand. Specifi-

---

1. The model developed here is essentially that first presented by Dixit and Stiglitz (1977). In this model the possibility of product differentiation arises from the desire of every individual to consume a variety of goods, an approach also taken by Spence (1976). An alternative and more realistic formulation is to suppose that individuals have different tastes and that goods with different characteristics aim to satisfy this variety of tastes; this approach is identified with Lancaster (1980). Applications of the Lancasterian approach to tariff analysis, however, present severe technical difficulties; see Lancaster (1984).

cally, we assume that each individual's tastes are represented by the utility function

$$U = \left[\sum_{i=1}^{n} D_i^{\alpha} \right]^{1/\alpha}, \qquad 0 < \alpha < 1, \tag{7.1}$$

where D_i is consumption of the ith product and n is the number of available products.

The utility function (7.1) has some very convenient properties. The elasticity of substitution between any two products—or any two groups of products—is $\sigma = 1/(1 - \alpha) > 1$. The demand for any individual product i takes the form

$$D_i = D \left(\frac{p_i}{P} \right)^{-\sigma}, \tag{7.2}$$

where

$$D = \left[\sum_{i} D_i^{\alpha} \right]^{1/\alpha}, \tag{7.3}$$

$$P = \left[\sum_{i} p_i^{\alpha/(\alpha-1)} \right]^{(\alpha-1)/\alpha}, \tag{7.4}$$

and p_i represents the price of variety i; D may be interpreted as an index of total consumption, and P is an index of the price level. The important implication of (7.2) is the following: if a single firm produces a good i, and that firm is small enough relative to the economy as a whole that it regards itself as unable to affect D or P, then it will view itself as facing a demand curve of elasticity σ.

Turning next to the production side, we assume that the economy has only one factor of production. To produce a good in a quantity x requires a labor input $g(x)$. There are assumed to be economies of scale so that $g(x)/x$ is declining in x—average labor input per unit is lower, the larger is production.

Because there are economies of scale, there will be imperfect competition. Because there are a large number of symmetric potential products, however, there is no reason for two firms to try to produce the same good. Thus the market structure will be monopolistically competitive: each good that is produced will be produced by a single firm.

The pricing decision of an individual firm is that of a monopolist: set marginal revenue equal to marginal cost. Marginal cost for firm i

is $wg'(x_i)$, where w is the wage rate. Marginal revenue is $p_i(\sigma - 1)/\sigma$. Thus the pricing rule is

$$p_i = \frac{wg'(x_i)\sigma}{\sigma - 1},$$

or

$$\frac{p_i}{w} = \frac{g'(x_i)\sigma}{\sigma - 1}. \tag{7.5}$$

An additional condition on pricing arises from the possibility of entry or exit by firms. Absent any restrictions on entry and exit, profits will be competed away, implying a price equal to average cost:

$$\frac{p_i}{w} = \frac{g(x_i)}{x_i}. \tag{7.6}$$

The conditions (7.5) and (7.6) together jointly determine the price and output of the representative firm. In figure 7.1 the curve PP represents the pricing condition (7.5) and ZZ represents the zero-profit condition (7.6); their intersection determines the equilibrium. Notice that the figure is drawn with PP downward sloping, which would be the case if marginal cost is declining in output. This need not be the case. Clearly, however, the results would be unaffected if PP were flat or upward sloping.[2] The intersection of the two curves determines output per firm and price relative to the wage rate; they

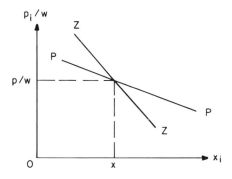

Figure 7.1

2. When PP slopes downward, we require it to be flatter than ZZ.

are the same for all goods. The only remaining question is the number of goods produced. Denote this number by n, and the economy's labor force by L. Then the number of goods actually produced is determined by full employment:

$$n = \frac{L}{g(x)},$$ (7.7)

where x is taken from figure 7.1

Which n goods are produced? The model does not tell us. Since all the goods are symmetric, it makes no difference, however.

7.2 Tariffs and the Terms of Trade

Now consider a world consisting of two economies like the one described in section 7.1; call them Home and Foreign. We suppose that the two economies have the same tastes, that is, that (7.1) applies to both (it does not matter whether the technologies are the same).

Home and Foreign are able to trade with each other. There may be transport costs; if there are, they take the form of "iceberg" costs in which a fraction ϕ of any good melts away in transit. This has the effect of driving a constant proportional wedge between the FOB price of a good and the price in the other country. Thus let p_H be the price of a representative Home good in its domestic market, and let p_F be the price of the same good in the Foreign market. Then

$$p_F = (1 + \phi)p_H.$$ (7.8)

Similarly, if p_H^* is the price of a representative Foreign good in Home's market, we have

$$p_H^* = (1 + \phi)p_F^*,$$ (7.9)

where p_F^* denotes the price of a foreign good in the foreign market.

This assumption about the form of transport costs has a key useful implication: since the price of a good in the export market is proportional to the domestic price and since the utility function (7.1) implies constant elasticity demands, the *overall* demand also has constant elasticity σ. Thus the pricing rule (7.5) still holds. Since the zero-profit condition (7.6) is unchanged, the result is that international trade has no effect on either the output or the markup of a representative firm—and thus no effect on the number of goods produced in each country.

In our trading world, then, we have Home producing n goods and Foreign producing n^* different goods. Given the taste of each consumer for variety, each will consume some of the other's products. That is, there will be intraindustry trade.

Although the origin of trade lies in economies of scale, what we effectively have is a situation in which each country is specialized in producing different things. Specifically, Home is producing one composite commodity consisting of its n goods, and Foreign a different composite commodity consisting of its n^* goods. These composite commodities are imperfect substitutes, with an elasticity of substitution in demand equal to σ.

Now, finally, we are prepared to consider trade policy. In particular, consider the welfare effects of an ad valorem tariff rate τ imposed by Home. Does this improve Home's welfare?

Like the iceberg transport costs, an ad valorem tariff does not affect the elasticity of demand faced by an individual producer. Thus the number of goods produced in each country remains unchanged, and the two countries remain effectively specialized in the production of different composite commodities. This means that the effect of a tariff is the same as would be the case if the two countries were specialized due to comparative advantage rather than economies of scale.

This means that we can directly apply the analysis of an optimal tariff in a competitive market setting developed in chapter 2. We note first that a small tariff definitely benefits Home. A tariff's costs consist of the distortion of consumption choices, but its benefits take the form of an improvement in the terms of trade. The benefit, however, is first order in the tariff rate, whereas the costs are second order. Thus a small tariff raises welfare.

What about the optimal tariff? We know from chapter 2 that the optimal tariff can be represented as a function of the Foreign elasticity of import demand, namely [see (2.3)],

$$\bar{\tau} = \frac{1}{\epsilon^* - 1}. \tag{7.10}$$

To determine the elasticity of Foreign import demand, we start with the Foreign budget identity:

$$n p_F d_H^* + n^* p_F^* d_F^* = n^* p_F^* x^*,$$

where n and n^* are the number of goods produced in Home and Foreign, respectively, p_F and p_F^* are the prices in Foreign of representative Home and Foreign goods, d_H^* and d_F^* are Foreign consumption of each Home and Foreign good, and x^* is the output of each Foreign good. If we define $p^* = p_F/p_F^*$, the relative price of imports, we can simplify to

$$np d_H^* + n^* d_F^* = n^* x^*. \tag{7.11}$$

Now consider a tariff-induced changed in p. We know that the tariff does not affect n, n^*, or x. Thus it must be true that

$$s_H^* \hat{d}_H^* + s_F^* \hat{d}_F^* = - s_H^* \hat{p}^*, \tag{7.12}$$

where a "hat" indicates a proportional rate of change and s_i^* denotes an expenditure share on country i goods.

Since σ is the elasticity of substitution between Home and Foreign products [see (7.2)], we have

$$\hat{d}_H^* - \hat{d}_F^* = - \sigma \hat{p}^*. \tag{7.13}$$

By substituting (7.13) back into (7.12) and rearranging, we get

$$\hat{d}_H^* = - (s_H^* + s_F^* \sigma) \hat{p}^*. \tag{7.14}$$

The bracketed expression in (7.14) is therefore the elasticity of import demand.

Finally, we substitute back into the optimal tariff formula (7.10) to derive the optimal tariff:

$$\bar{\tau} = \frac{1}{s_F^*(\sigma - 1)}. \tag{7.15}$$

What does (7.15) tell us? The share s_F^* is clearly related to the relative economic size of Home. If Home is a small country, accounting for only a small fraction of gross world product, s_F^* will be near 1. What the formula therefore tells us is that the larger Home bulks in the world economy (the smaller s_F^* is), the higher is its optimal tariff rate. This is not surprising—we expect small countries to have less scope for optimal tariffs than large countries.

What is surprising is the point emphasized by Gros (1987): the optimal tariff never goes to zero, no matter how small the country. Even a country that is very small in the world economy, and that therefore accounts for a negligible share of the rest of the world's expenditure, still has an optimal tariff rate of $1/(\sigma - 1)$.

There are two ways to interpret this result. Both are correct, but they shed light on the problem from different directions.

One interpretation is to note that in a monopolistically competitive world there are no price-takers. No matter how small a country is, it is still specialized in a range of products that nobody else produces and is therefore a price-setter that can influence its terms of trade. A small country is not small in the sense that it is a price-taker on world markets.

The alternative interpretation would stress the role of imperfect competition. Compare (7.15) with (7.5): the optimal tariff for a very small country is the same as the markup over marginal cost. This is not an accident. The true cost of domestic products to a country is their marginal cost, which in a monopolistically competitive world is less than their market price. Meanwhile the true cost of imported goods is their market price plus any effect of additional demand on that price. In a small country this last effect is negligible, so the true cost of imports is simply the market price. To give domestic consumers the right signal, then, domestic goods must be made to seem relatively cheaper compared with imports. A tariff accomplishes this.

In the context of this model, these two views of the reasons for the small country's optimal tariff are equally valid. However, the imperfect competition view is broader in its implications, for it may apply even where there is no possibility of altering the terms of trade. In the next section we turn to a slightly modified model that makes this point.

7.3 The Production Efficiency Effect

We argued in the previous section that a possible way to think about the reasons for a positive optimal tariff, even for a small country, is the benefit from increasing demand for domestically produced goods whose price exceeds marginal cost. To bring out this point more clearly, we now modify our model in such a way as to eliminate the conventional terms of trade effects of a tariff.

We do this by introducing an additional, "outside," good that is produced with constant returns to scale. Trade in this outside good ties down the terms of trade, leaving difference between price and marginal cost as the only source of possible benefit from a tariff.

We suppose, then, that there are two industries: the differentiated product industry, and a constant return sector producing the outside good Y. Tastes are assumed represented by

$$U = A\theta^{-1}D^{\theta} + Y, \qquad 0 < \theta < 1, \tag{7.16}$$

where D is an index of consumption of the differentiated products, defined as in (7.3) and Y is consumption of the outside good. We thus assume for simplicity that utility is linear in terms of the outside good so that there are no income effects on the demand for the differentiated product.

A consumer maximizing (7.16) will set

$$AD^{\theta-1} = P,$$

where P is the price index of the differentiated product sector in terms of the outside good, or

$$D = (A^{-1}P)^{-1/(1-\theta)} = BP^{-\epsilon}, \qquad \epsilon = \frac{1}{1 - \theta}.$$

Using (7.2), we therefore have

$$D_i = Bp_i^{-\sigma}P^{\sigma-\epsilon}. \tag{7.17}$$

That is, demand for any individual good depends on both its own price in terms of the outside good and on the overall price index in terms of that good. So long as $\sigma > \epsilon$—that is, so long as the elasticity of substitution within the sector is larger than the overall price elasticity—the demand for an individual good will depend positively on the overall price index. We will henceforth assume this to be the case.

We now assume that there are two factors of production. One factor, which we will call unskilled labor and denote as L, is used in both the differentiated product sector and in the Y-sector. The other factor, which we will refer to as "skilled labor" and denote as K, is used only in the D-sector. Specifically, we assume that in the production of the outside good there are constant returns to scale, with a unit labor requirement a_{LY} that is independent of the scale of production. In the differentiated product sector there is also a constant unit labor requirement a_{LD}. There is a fixed cost, however, that consists entirely of skilled labor: it requires k units of skilled labor to produce a differentiated product at all, with this labor requirement independent of the quantity produced.

Before turning to trade, we note the implications of this setup for the equilibrium in a single economy. The outside good will, of course, necessarily be priced at marginal (which is also average) cost:

$$p_Y = w_L a_{LY}, \tag{7.18}$$

where w_L is the wage rate of unskilled labor.

The representative differentiated product will be priced as a markup over marginal cost. As long as there are many such goods produced, the elasticity of demand facing each individual producer will still be approximately σ, so the pricing rule in this sector is

$$p_D = \frac{w_L a_{LD} \sigma}{\sigma - 1} . \tag{7.19}$$

Now price must still equal average cost. However, the number of firms is no longer the adjusting variable. The reason is that in order to start a firm one needs k units of skilled labor, and there is a limited suppy of that labor. So what happens, instead, is that the supply of skilled labor determines how many differentiated products are produced, and the wage rate of skilled labor adjusts so as to ensure zero profits. That is, the number of differentiated goods produced must be

$$n = \frac{K}{k} , \tag{7.20}$$

where K is the supply of skilled labor, and the wage rate of skilled labor must satisfy

$$w_H k = p_D x - w_L a_{LD} x, \tag{7.21}$$

where x is the output of a representative product. In effect, the operating surplus of firms, the difference between their revenues and their variable costs, is divided up among the skilled workers.

Now let us consider two economies of this type that are trading with each other. Assume that this trade can occur costlessly and that in an equilibrium both countries do produce some of the outside good Y. Then the price of Y must be the same in both countries, and this ties down relative wage rates for unskilled labor:

$$\frac{w_L}{w_L^*} = \frac{a_{LY}^*}{a_{LY}} . \tag{7.22}$$

We also know, however, that in each country the price of representative differentiated products is proportional to the wage rate, so long as the elasticity of demand facing the representative firm does not change. Thus the relative producer prices of the differentiated products from each country are also tied down:

$$\frac{p_H}{p_F^*} = \left(\frac{a_{LD}}{a_{LD}^*}\right)\left(\frac{w_L}{w_L^*}\right) = \left(\frac{a_{LD}}{a_{LD}^*}\right)\left(\frac{a_{LY}^*}{a_{LY}}\right). \tag{7.23}$$

So in this setup an ad valorem tariff, which we saw in the model of the previous section turned out to be welfare improving because it improved the terms of trade, cannot have that effect. The presence of the outside good ties down not only the price of that good but the relative *producer* prices of differentiated products as well. Nevertheless, a tariff can improve a country's welfare.

To see why, let's think about what happens if Home imposes a very small tariff against Foreign differentiated products (*not* against the outside good). This will have three important effects: (1) it will raise the consumer price of imported differentiated products in terms of other goods (and also in terms of the wages of unskilled labor), (2) it will generate revenue, and (3) it will induce substitution on the part of Home consumers. Faced with a higher relative price of imported differentiated goods, these consumers will switch demand within the set of differentiated products from imported to domestic goods.

What are the welfare effects of these three changes? As the analysis in chapter 2 showed, for a small tariff (1) and (2) will just exactly cancel out—the revenue from a tariff will be just enough to compensate consumers for the rise in prices that the tariff causes. What we are left with, then, is the rise in demand for domestic goods. Since prices are tied down, the output of a representative differentiated good, x, must increase. This means a larger operating surplus, and thus a higher wage rate for skilled labor [see (7.21)]. There is no offsetting loss. So the small tariff increases welfare for the country as a whole (see Flam and Helpman 1987 for a more general analysis).

The point here is, of course, that the marginal cost of a unit of D produced at home is less than its price, so domestic consumers consume too little. A tariff can serve as a way to increase domestic consumption of domestically produced D and can therefore raise real national income. This shows that the potential case for protection in a monopolistically competitive world is not simply the standard argument for tariffs that improve the importer's terms of trade.

This model can also be used to make some of the points about trade war that we discussed in section 5.6 of chapter 5. Suppose for a moment that the two countries are symmetric and that both of them impose tariffs at equal rates in an effort to switch demand from foreign to domestic goods. What will be the net effect? Any switching of domestic consumers away from imported D will be offset, for each country, by an equal loss of exports. Meanwhile, by raising the prices of imports, the two governments will induce consumers to switch away from differentiated products generally toward the constant returns sector. The result will be to lower the wages of skilled labor in both countries, without any compensating benefit. That is, this is a model in which protection is in the interest of each country acting unilaterally but is destructive if both practice it at the same time.

More fundamentally, however, we should notice that tariffs are a second-best policy in any case. The real distortion here is that domestic consumers do not act on the basis of the true social marginal cost of domestic output. The correct policy is really to subsidize domestic consumption of domestic differentiated goods.

In particular, suppose that all domestic consumption of domestic D were to receive a proportional subsidy at the rate $1/(\sigma - 1)$, so that the price to domestic consumers is just equal to marginal cost. What would happen if a small tariff were imposed? As before, the tariff would generate an increase in the price of imports, just offset by the tariff revenue. It would also generate an increase in the operating surplus of domestic firms, which would be captured by the wage rate of skilled labor. However, there would now be a fourth effect: an increase in subsidy payments for domestic consumption. This increase in subsidy costs would just equal the gain in operating surplus, since we have assumed that the subsidy is precisely equal to the difference between price and marginal cost. So there would be no net gain from the tariff.

In other words, the apparent case for protection here is really based on a domestic distortion—the divergence between consumer prices and marginal costs—and the case for a tariff disappears when this distortion is addressed directly. As we will see in chapter 8, empirical work on trade policy in imperfectly competitive industries often leads to the result that as a greater range of policy instruments becomes available, the appropriate policy looks less and less like a trade policy per se. This model helps to suggest why.

In any case we have now seen that divergence between price and marginal cost can give rise to at least a second-best case for a tariff even when the terms of trade cannot be changed. We now turn to a surprising and interesting possibility that has emerged from studying models of this type: that a tariff not only can improve the terms of trade but can even lower prices in the domestic market.

7.4 Tariffs That Lower Prices: The Home Market Effect

The idea that a tariff can actually lower prices in the domestic market sounds paradoxical. After all, a tariff is in the first instance a tax, and this surely ought to tend to raise prices. Although conventional analysis does allow for taxes that lower prices when there are backward-bending supply curves, such cases are normally regarded as curiosa rather than as illustrating any fundamental principle. The possibility of a price-lowering tariff, by contrast, arises from some more fundamental considerations involving the interaction between increasing returns and transportation costs.

It may be useful to consider an extreme suggestive example to understand how a tariff can lower prices, before proceeding to a formal model. Imagine that there is some good that can be produced in either of two countries at roughly the same cost. There are substantial costs to transporting the good between the two countries; however, there are also large economies of scale in production, sufficient to ensure that the good will be produced in only one country despite these transport costs. Thus one country will end up producing the good and exporting it to the other.

Now it seems evident that consumers in whichever country actually gets to produce the good will pay a lower price for the good than their counterparts in the other since they will not have to pay for shipping. In principle, if one country—say, country A—has a small advantage (either slightly lower production costs or a slightly larger market), this could translate into a substantial secondary benefit from lower prices.

But now suppose that country B imposes a tariff on imports of the good from country A. This will change the relative advantage of locating production in the two nations. If a firm produces the good in A, it must pay the tariff in order to sell its goods in B, but if a firm produces the good in B, it will not have to pay any corresponding cost to sell in A. So if the countries have markets of similar size, if they can produce at a similar cost and if the tariff is large enough, the result of a tariff will be to induce production in B instead of A.

But this will actually lower the price of the good to B's consumers because they will no longer have to pay the shipping charges. So a tariff, by shifting the location of production, can actually lower consumer prices!

So much for the intuition. To solidify our grasp of the idea, we need a fully worked-out model. We do this by combining features from the models of sections 7.2 and 7.3, leading to a variant on a model that was developed by Venables (1987).

Consider, then, a two-country world in which there is both a differentiated-product sector and a homogeneous outside good, as in section 7.3. Demand for the two goods is represented by equation (7.16). However, we now return to the assumption that there is only one factor of production, labor, that can be used to produce either the outside good Y (at constant returns) or the differentiated goods that make up D (at increasing returns). Thus the number of goods is once again variable, and firms will enter until profits are driven to zero.

We continue to assume that the outside good can be traded costlessly, tying down the relative wage rates of the two counties. But we now allow once again for some "iceberg" transportation costs, at a rate ϕ, for shipments of the differentiated product. This has the effect of making the pattern of consumption somewhat different between the two countries: each country spends relatively more on differentiated products produced domestically than the other does. Or, to put it another way, the Home market is more important to the representative Home producer than it is to the representative Foreign producer.

As we know from the discussion in previous sections, quite a few aspects of the international equilibrium can be tied down by looking at the structure of the model. In particular, the relative wage rate of the two countries is tied down by the fact that the outside good is traded [see (7.22)], and we know both the output of a representative differentiated product and the producer price of differentiated products in terms of labor, and thus also in terms of the outside good [see (7.5) and (7.6)]. Let $\bar{x}$ denote the equilibrium output per firm, and let p denote the price of a differentiated product in terms of the outside good. We assume that both countries have the same tech-nologies. Therefore x and p are the same in both.

Now transport costs have two effects. First, they raise the relative price of imports; under free trade the consumer price of an imported good will be $p(1 + \phi)$. Second, they generate an indirect demand for goods that "melt away" in transportation. Bearing these two points in mind, the market-clearing condition for a Home firm may be written

$$\bar{x} = Bp^{-\sigma}P^{\sigma-\epsilon} + (1 + \phi)^{1-\sigma}B^*p^{-\sigma}(P^*)^{\sigma-\epsilon}, \tag{7.24}$$

where B and B^* are the constants from the Home and Foreign utility functions; P and P^* are the consumer price indexes for differentiated products in each country. Similarly, the market-clearing condition for a Foreign firm may be written

$$\bar{x} = (1 + \phi)^{1-\sigma}Bp^{-\sigma}P^{\sigma-\epsilon} + B^*p^{-\sigma}(P^*)^{\sigma-\epsilon}. \tag{7.25}$$

The two conditions are illustrated in figure 7.2 whose axes represent possible values of $P^{\sigma-\epsilon}$ and $(P^*)^{\sigma-\epsilon}$, that is, transformations of the consumer price indexes for differentiated products in each country (see Venables 1987). The schedule HH corresponds to (7.24); FF corresponds to (7.25). Point 1 represents the equilibrium. The slopes of the two schedules are apparent from inspection of the equations: HH has a slope of $B/B^*(1 + \phi)^{1-\sigma}$, and FF the flatter slope $B(1 + \phi)^{1-\sigma}/B^*$. The intuition behind these relative slopes is as follows: since firms do not have to pay transport costs to sell in their

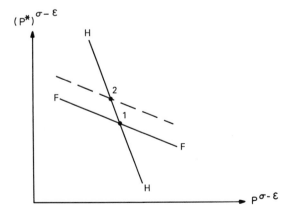

Figure 7.2

domestic market, the local market is relatively more important to each country's firms than it is to firms based abroad. A fall in P cuts relatively more into the sales of Home firms than Foreign and must be offset by a larger rise in P^* to keep sales unchanged.

What adjusts to produce this equilibrium? The answer is the number of firms active in each country. As we move southeast along either schedule, we are imagining a redistribution of production from Home to Foreign that makes Home consumers worse off (because they must pay transport costs on more of their consumption) and Foreign consumers better off (because their own shipping charges are reduced). This one sees from (7.4), which implies that

$$\frac{P^{-\alpha/(1-\alpha)}}{p^{-\alpha/(1-\alpha)}} = n + n^*(1 + \phi)^{-\alpha/(1-\alpha)},$$

$$\frac{(P^*)^{-\alpha/(1-\alpha)}}{p^{-\alpha/(1-\alpha)}} = n(1 + \phi)^{-\alpha/(1-\alpha)} + n^*.$$

In fact, having calculated the equilibrium consumer price indexes, we can use these two equations to calculate the equilibrium number of firms in each country.

Now consider what happens if Home imposes an ad valorem tariff, at the rate τ, on imports of differentiated products but not on the outside good. This has the effect of raising the price that Home consumers must pay for foreign differentiated imports from $p(1 + \phi)$ to $p(1 + \phi)(1 + \tau)$. Accordingly, the market-clearing condition for Foreign firms becomes

$$\bar{x} = (1 + \phi)^{1-\sigma}(1 + \tau)^{-\sigma}Bp^{-\sigma}P^{\sigma-\epsilon} + B^*p^{-\sigma}(P^*)^{\sigma-\epsilon}. \tag{7.26}$$

Clearly, demand will be reduced for any given (P, P^*); to offset this, one or both price indexes must rise. So the result is to shift the *FF* schedule out. The equilibrium in figure 7.2 thus shifts from point 1 to point 2.

But we now see the point that we argued intuitively at the beginning of this section. The imposition of a tariff actually lowers the price index faced by Home consumers (while raising that faced by Foreign consumers). The reason is the home market effect in which a protected market becomes a favored place to produce to serve the unprotected market as well. Home welfare clearly rises. The gains result from a change in the composition of variety that is favorable to Home consumers; they obtain more cheaper Home products and fewer expensive foreign products. Their overall cost of these products per unit real income declines.

The idea that a tariff can actually lower average consumer prices is a fairly remarkable one, so it is probably worth pointing out its limitations. The chief one is quantitative. A tariff only lowers prices when firms produce in both countries both before and after the tariff change. Yet, unless there are large transportation costs, this can be true only for a modest tariff rate. On the other hand, when transportation costs are large, there will not be much intraindustry trade, and thus little prospect for gain from a tariff, unless there are also very large economies of scale. So the prospect for lowering price through protection, though not exactly a pure curiosum, will be meaningful in a practical sense only where large transport costs are combined with large-scale economies—not, one guesses, an extensive set of industries.

7.5 Tariffs and Segmented Markets

We mentioned at the start of this chapter that there are two theories of intraindustry trade—one that emphasizes increasing returns plus product differentiation, and one that relies, instead, on market segmentation and price discrimination. Thus far we have focused entirely on the product differentiation case; now we turn to market segmentation. As we will see, here the home market effect of a tariff comes through even more strongly. A tariff not only shifts production to the domestic market, and thereby lowers the price index for domestic consumers, it may actually lower the prices charged by domestic firms.

As a first step we need to state the basic segmented market model of trade. This model was first proposed by Brander (1981) and elaborated by Brander and Krugman (1983); we have elsewhere given it a compact statement (Helpman and Krugman 1985). We will therefore be brief here. We imagine two countries that both demand some homogeneous good and that are both able to produce it; for the sake of simplicity we assume that the countries are symmetric, although this is not necessary for the results. The demand in either country may be written in inverse form as

$$p_j = p(Q_j), \qquad j = H, F, \tag{7.27}$$

where p is the price in that market, Q is total deliveries to that market, and the subscripts H and F refer to the two countries.

The costs of a firm are assumed to take the linear form

$$C(x, y) = k + cx + c(1 + \phi)y, \tag{7.28}$$

where x is a firm's deliveries to the domestic market and y is the firms's export sales. That is, the firm has a fixed cost, constant marginal production cost c, and faces a transportation cost for exports at the rate ϕ. We assume that an individual firm can decide how much of its output to sell in each market—that is, it can price discriminate, charging a different price net of transport costs for exports than it does on domestic sales.

Since competition among firms may take place in two markets, it is essential to make some assumption about how the two markets interact. The key assumption is that each firm plays separate Cournot games in each market, taking not only the output levels of other firms as given but also the division of their output between the two markets as given. This assumption is not fully satisfactory, as we will discuss shortly. For now, however, let us explore that assumption's implications.

A good way to start is to ask what would happen if there were n firms in each market and there were no trade in this good. As we know, in an n-firm Cournot oligopoly there will be a perceived marginal revenue curve that lies between the true industry marginal revenue and the demand curve, and perceived marginal revenue will equal marginal cost. Thus

$$p(Q) + p'(Q)\left(\frac{Q}{n}\right) = c,$$

or

$$p - c = -p'(Q)\left(\frac{Q}{n}\right) \tag{7.29}$$

in both markets. In other words, in both markets price will exceed marginal cost by an amount that reflects the perceived effect of increased output on the price of inframarginal sales.

Now suppose that we allow the possibility of trade. A firm that considers exporting knows that it will have to incur a higher marginal cost, $c(1 + \phi)$. However, if a firm is not initially exporting, it has no inframarginal units in the foreign market. So on its first unit of sales the firm will consider itself to face a marginal revenue that is the same as the price. Thus starting from a no-trade equilibrium, exporting from Home will appear profitable so long as $p_F > c(1 + \phi)$. If p_F and p_H are the same, this is equivalent to

$$p - c = - p'(Q) \left(\frac{Q}{n}\right) > c\phi.$$

That is, some exporting will appear profitable so long as the markup of price over marginal cost in the absence of trade exceeds the cost of transportation.

The interesting point is that if this criterion is satisfied, exports will occur in *both* directions: even as Home firms export to Foreign, Foreign firms will export to Home. This is the phenomenon of "reciprocal dumping" in which each country's firms absorb transport costs in order to sell in the other country's market.

In a trade equilibrium perceived marginal revenue must equal marginal costs in both markets. For a Home firm, the equilibrium conditions are

$$p_H + xp'(Q_H) = c \tag{7.30}$$

in the domestic market, and

$$p_F + yp'(Q_F) = c(1 + \phi) \tag{7.31}$$

in the export market.

A useful point to notice is that these equilibrium conditions in effect determine the firm's sales in each market as a function of the price in each market. To see this, notice that the inverse demand function (7.27) may be inverted to define $Q = Q(p)$. Then (7.30) may be rewritten as

$$p_H + xp'[Q(p_H)] = c,$$

and similarly for (7.31). This then defines x as a function of p_H, $x(p_H)$. Ordinarily, this function increases in p_H.[3] We define $y(p_F)$ in a similar way.

Now let us turn to the question of entry. If there is free entry (and

---

3. We have $\partial x/\partial p_H = -(1 + xp''/p')/p'$. The denominator is necessarily negative. The term in brackets will be positive as long as xp''/p' is not too negative. In particular, for the case of a linear demand curve $\partial x/\partial p_H$ is always positive.

if, as usual, we ignore the fact that the number of firms must be an integer), then profits will be driven to zero. The zero-profit condition for a Home firm is

$$p_H x(p_H) + p_F y(p_F) = k + cx(p_H) + c(1 + \phi)y(p_F), \quad \text{or}$$

$$(p_H - c)x(p_H) + [p_F - c(1 + \phi)]y(p_F) = k. \tag{7.32}$$

That is, the operating surplus equals fixed costs. Since $x(\cdot)$ and $y(\cdot)$ are normally increasing functions, operating surplus is also increasing in both prices, so (7.32) defines a downward-sloping schedule in (p_H, p_F) space, shown as HH in figure 7.3. Similarly, the zero-profit condition for a Foreign firm is shown as FF. The relatively greater importance of the Home market for a Home firm ensures that its operating surplus is relatively strongly affected by p_H compared with a Foreign firm, so HH is steeper than FF. The equilibrium is at point 1.

At this point the parallel with the analysis in section 7.4 is obvious, and so is the next step. Suppose that Home imposes a tariff—say, a specific tariff at a rate t—against imports from Foreign. From the point of view of Foreign firms, this has the same effect as if they were to face an increase in transportation costs. To cover fixed costs, they require higher prices in one or both markets: FF therefore shifts out, to $F'F'$.[4] The equilibrium shifts from 1 to 2. As before, a tariff

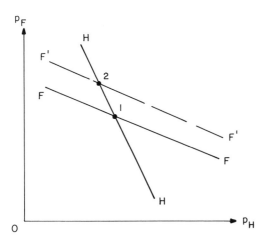

Figure 7.3

4. The tariff reduces every foreign firm's profit margin on Home sales as well as its

actually lowers the price in the domestic market. This time, however, the price on the axis is not only an index but the actual price charged by domestic firms (see Venables 1985).

How is this possible? The tariff, by making foreign production less profitable, induces exit by foreign firms; this means that the export market becomes more profitable to domestic firms. The result is entry at home. The surprising point is that the entry of additional domestic firms necessarily reduces the degree of market power of domestic firms in their home market despite the protection they receive from imports. Of course, the tariff is anticompetitive abroad; domestic consumers gain from increased exploitation of foreign consumers.

The caveats that we raised about the importance of the price-lowering effect of a tariff in the previous section apply with equal or perhaps even stronger force here. There are also some deeper questions. Is the segmented market model of trade employed in this section reasonable? It seems suitable for situations in which firms precommit output to specific markets. But often manufacturers with a limited capacity to produce are able to freely (although possibly at a cost) allocate goods across markets. In addition they also engage in some form of price competition. It is shown in Ben-Zvi and Helpman (1988) that when manufactures set prices before allocating goods across markets but after the determination of the capacity to produce, there will be no two-way trade in identical products. In this case our policy conclusions do not apply. The theory of oligopoly in segmented markets, important as it may be, has not been sufficiently developed to provide a reliable guide to policy analysis. For this reason our conclusions are only tentative.

References

Ben-Zvi, Shmuel, and Helpman, Elhanan. (1988). "Oligopoly in segmented markets." NBER Working Paper No. 2665.

Brander, James. (1981). "Intra-industry trade in identical commodities." *Journal of International Economics* 11: 1–14.

Brander, James, and Krugman, Paul R. (1983). "A 'reciprocal dumping' model of international trade." *Journal of International Economics* 15: 313–321.

Dixit, Avinash K., and Stiglitz, Joseph (1977). "Monopolistic competition and optimum product diversity." *American Economic Review* 67: 297–308.

$x(\cdot)$ function. The FF curve shifts out for both reasons. This result applies to both specific and ad valorem tariffs.

Flam, Harry, and Helpman, Elhanan (1987). "Industrial policy under monopolistic competition." *Journal of International Economics* 22: 79–102.

Gros, Daniel (1987). "A note on the optimal tariff, retaliation and the welfare loss from tariff wars in a framework with intra-industry trade." *Journal of International Economics* 23: 357–367.

Helpman, Elhanan (1987). "Imperfect competition and international trade: evidence from fourteen industrial countries." *Journal of the Japanese and International Economies* 1: 62–81.

Helpman, Elhanan, and Krugman, Paul R. (1985). *Market Structure and Foreign Trade*. Cambridge, MA: MIT Press.

Lancaster, Kelvin (1984). "Protection and product differentiation." In Henryk Kierzkowski (ed.), *Monopolistic Competition and International Trade*. Oxford: Clarendon Press.

Venables, Anthony J. (1985). "Trade and trade policy with imperfect competition: The case of identical products and free entry." *Journal of International Economics* 19: 1–20.

Venables, Anthony J. (1987). "Trade and trade policy with differentiated products: A Chamberlinian-Ricardian model." *Economic Journal* 97: 700–717.

8   Quantification

Up to this point, our analysis has been entirely theoretical. This
abstractness is not a matter of preference, but one of necessity. Unfortunately, there does not yet exist a large body of empirical work
on trade in imperfectly competitive markets, on which we could draw
for our work. Indeed, empirical work in this area has emerged only
slowly because of the difficulties that will become apparent in this
chapter's discussion.

Nevertheless, there is now a significant and growing empirical
literature on trade policy under imperfect competition, and this literature has had a significant impact on some real-world policy de-
bates. The purpose of this chapter is to explain the principles
underlying the new empirical literature and to survey briefly some
of the more prominent efforts.

We begin by illustrating the principles and problems of the new
literature by considering the problem of quantification in a hypothetical, simplified oligopolistic industry. We then turn to the three
main variants of quantitative models in the new literature: those in
which the number of firms is taken to be fixed, those in which free
entry is assumed to compete away all profits, and the efforts at
general equilibrium analysis.

8.1 Problems of Quantification

Most of the problems of quantification in the new trade theory are
not specific to trade per se. Instead, they are the generic problems
of modeling imperfectly competitive industries. If the issue of quantification has become most acute in the trade literature, it is because
the practical question of how an imperfectly competitive industry will
respond to an industry-specific change in incentives seems to be

more usual in trade policy than in regulation or antitrust. Since the conceptual issues are not specific to trade, however, it is actually more convenient to begin by thinking about a simple domestic oligopoly that does not face international competition.

Consider, then, an oligopolistic industry consisting of n firms. In general, we may suppose that the firms produce differentiated products; the case of a homogeneous product may be taken as a special case. Let us also suppose that we are prepared to regard the firms as symmetric, that is, to think in terms of a representative firm. Obviously, this will not be the case in fact: in reality industries contain a wide range of firm sizes and experiences. However, the normal practice in empirical work to date has been to squeeze the actual data into a symmetric-firm mold. We will examine the (unsatisfactory) ways in which this may be done later, but for now we will suppose that this has somehow been done.

What do we actually observe when we look at data on such an industry? All that we can directly observe is the output per firm x and the price charged by the representative firm p. In order to perform comparative statics on a model of the industry, however, we need three more kinds of information. These are (1) the demand curve, (2) the cost function of the representative firm, and (3) the industry's *conduct*—how firms compete with one another.

The need for (1) and (2) is no different from what is needed to perform comparative statics on a competitive industry and may be approached in the same way. Demand curves may be estimated econometrically using time series data. Costs may similarly be estimated econometrically or by an engineering approach. There are well-known pitfalls in these procedures. Still, the special problem of imperfect competition arises from the need to model industry conduct.

The first key decision in modeling industry conduct is whether to regard firms as acting cooperatively or noncooperatively. In reality, some tacit collusion is a feature of many oligopolies. However, as we saw in earlier chapters, models of collusive behavior still leave much to be desired. Though we will briefly discuss some recent efforts at tackling the reality of collusion in this section, the usual response to date has been to model industries as if they were noncooperative.

Now even if an industry behaves in a noncooperative fashion, the outcome depends on the strategy space in which firms compete. Throughout our theoretical analysis, we have focused on the two cases of competition in prices—Bertrand competition—and competition in quantities—Cournot competition. The essential problem in quantifying real industries is that typically neither of these forms of competition works very well at explaining actual prices. The problem is therefore one of either specifying a form of market conduct that does accord with the data actually observed, or of revising other parts of the model to make sense of the observed data given an assumption about conduct.

The Key Role of Perceived Marginal Revenue

In noncooperative industries, conduct affects equilibrium pricing in helping to determine the difference between the marginal revenue perceived by a firm and the "true" marginal revenue facing an industry. The essential problem in modeling real industries quantitatively is to reverse this logic: to use the actual prices of an industry to infer the conduct of firms.

To facilitate the discussion, let us write the demand curve facing a representative firm in two ways. One way is to write price as a function of the firm's sales and of a price index of other firms:

$$p_i = p^B(x_i, P_i), \tag{8.1}$$

where $P_i = \Phi(p_1, \ldots, p_{i-1}, p_{i+1}, \ldots, p_n)$ denotes the price index of other firms; the other is as a function of the firm's sales and of an index of the sales of other firms:

$$p_i = p^C(x_i, X_i), \tag{8.2}$$

where $X_i = \Gamma(x_1, \ldots, x_{i-1}, x_{i+1}, \ldots, x_n)$ is the index of other firms' average sales.[1] The function $p^B(\cdot)$ is most useful for analyzing competition where firms play Bertrand, and p^C is most useful when firms play Cournot. However, since these functions are alternative statements of an underlying demand function, they are related to one another. In particular, we know that

$$p^B(x, p) = p^C(x, x) \tag{8.3}$$

---

1. We make assumptions about $\Gamma(\cdot)$ parallel to those made about $\Phi(\cdot)$: it is assumed to be linearly homogeneous in its arguments and scaled so that $\Gamma(x, \ldots, x) = x$. Also note that the case of a homogeneous product can be represented by $\Gamma(\cdot) = \Sigma_{j\neq i} x_j/(n-1)$.

defines the pari passu demand function. We also know that in a symmetrical equilibrium x_i and p_i lie on the pari passu demand curve and that

$$-p_x^B \le -p_x^C. \tag{8.4}$$

That is, the slope of the ceteris paribus demand curve for a single firm when other firms hold their prices constant is less steep than when they hold sales constant—because in the latter case an increase in one firm's sales drives down the prices of substitute products, magnifying the firm's own decline in price.

Now suppose that we set out to model an industry. Ideally, our econometric work has given us an estimate of the demand curve that can be expressed in either of the forms $p^B(\cdot)$ or $p^C(\cdot)$, and we may also hope to have an estimate of the cost function of a representative firm that gives us a number for the marginal cost c. We observe directly the output x and price p of a representative firm. The only remaining task, then, is to decide what model of firms' conduct is appropriate.

It is immediately apparent what we would do if our models and empirical work were as good as we would like them to be. In equilibrium, marginal cost is equal to perceived marginal revenue. In Bertrand competition, perceived marginal revenue is equal to

$$\widetilde{MR}^B(x,\, p) = p + x p_x^B(x,\, p) \tag{8.5}$$

in a symmetrical equilibrium, where $p = p^B(x,\, p)$. In Cournot competition, perceived marginal revenue is equal to

$$\widetilde{MR}^C(x,\, x) = p^C(x,\, x) + x p_x^C(x,\, x) \tag{8.6}$$

in a symmetrical equilibrium which, by (8.4), is smaller. So we simply calculate these two possible perceived marginal revenues and ask which one is equal to marginal cost. If (8.5) equals marginal cost, then we conclude that the industry plays Bertrand. If (8.6) equals marginal cost, we conclude that the industry plays Cournot.

Of course it never works out like this. In practice, neither estimate of marginal revenue comes close to the estimate of marginal cost. The problem is therefore how to describe industry conduct in a way that is consistent with the data.

Two basic approaches have been tried in the existing literature. One is to specify conduct in a more complex way, the so-called conjectural variations approach. The other is to impose an assumption about conduct and revise the estimate of demand structure to rationalize the data. We consider each in turn.

The Conjectural Variations Approach

The conjectural variations approach assumes that firms, though not actually cooperating with each other, believe that their actions will change the behavior of other firms. Specifically, each firm believes that if it increases its output by one unit, the representative other firm will change its output by κ units. The parameter κ is the firm's *conjectural variation*; by allowing κ to vary, we allow for a variety of possible industry conducts.

It is immediately apparent that a conjectural variations approach encompasses Bertrand and Cournot conduct as special cases. Cournot behavior is the case where $\kappa = 0$—where each firm takes other firms' output as given. Bertrand behavior is a little more complex to specify but may be understood by noting that the demand curve facing an individual firm under the conjectural variations approach has the slope

$$p_x^C(x, X) + \kappa p_X^C(x, X).$$

This will have the same slope as the demand curve under Bertrand behavior $p_x^B(x, P)$ when

$$\kappa = \frac{p_x^C - p_x^B}{p_X^C} < 0.$$

That is, Bertrand conduct may be viewed as arising when each firm believes that when it increases its output by one unit, other firms will cut their output by just enough to keep their own prices constant (see, for example, Eaton and Grossman 1986).

Since the conjectural variation parameter κ can range across a continuum of values, the empirical modeler can allow it to be chosen by the requirement that perceived marginal revenue equals marginal cost. Perceived marginal revenue under the conjectural variation approach is

$$\widetilde{MR}(x, X, \kappa) = p^C(x, X) + x\{p_x^C(x, X) + \kappa p_X^C(x, X)\}, \qquad (8.7a)$$

and we have

$$\widetilde{MR}(x, X, \kappa) = c. \tag{8.7b}$$

Given estimates of the demand curve and of marginal cost, this allows us to solve for κ.

The simplicity of this procedure is appealing, and conjectural variations remain a popular modeling tool. However, there are some deep objections to the concept, which have troubled all researchers in this area and appear to be leading to a preference for alternative techniques (see Tirole 1988, ch. 6).

The first objection is that the conjectural variations approach seems to be an awkward compromise between static and dynamic analysis. A Nash equilibrium in either the Bertrand or Cournot case can be thought of as the outcome of a game in which firms are obliged to choose quantities or prices simultaneously and independently. To caricature the process, we may imagine that corporate boards meet simultaneously on January 1 to set prices for the year. Each board goes through an exercise of the following kind: "If they think that we'll charge $4, then they'll want to charge $3.50, but that would only make it worth our while to charge $3.25 . . . ," ending up with the argument "if they charge $2.75, our best move is to do the same; if we charge $2.75, their best move is to do the same; and they know this as well as we do, so we can indeed charge $2.75 in the expectation that they will too." That is, the Bertrand equilibrium (and similarly the Cournot equilibrium, if firms choose quantities instead of prices) can be thought of as the maximizing outcome of firms acting independently at a single instant. This may not be a realistic story, but it is consistent and grounded in maximization.

By contrast, the conjectural variations story involves arguments of the form "if we increase our output by 1 unit, *then* they will match half of our increase . . . ." That is, it is a story that must involve a sequence of decisions taken over time. But if this is the model, then it is important to make the dynamics explicit. Trying to squeeze the dynamic interactions of firms into a single-period equilibrium concept leads to a situation in which one does not know what is supposed to be happening, and the grounding in maximization is lost.

Because the conjectural variation parameter lacks any grounding in maximizing behavior, exercises in comparative statics become questionable. Suppose that we have fitted our model to an industry with the aid of an estimated value of κ that corresponds to neither the Cournot nor the Bertrand case. Now we try to ask how the outcome would have been different in the presence of some government policy—say a tariff or an import quota. What should we assume about κ in the new equilibrium? The normal procedure is to assume that κ remains unchanged. However, there is no reason to presume that this is the case. Since κ is not derived from demand or costs but rather depends on behavior, there is nothing to say how it may change.

This critique has not stopped a number of researchers from using the conjectural variations approach and from assuming a constant κ when they perform comparative statics. The justification is one of practical compromise: although the procedure raises serious doubts, it is tractable, and it may be hoped that it gives at least a helpful indication of what the effects of policy *might* be. However, the problems with the conjectural variations approach have also led to the development of an alternative approach to the same problem.

The Product Differentiation Approach

For our illustrative discussion, we have assumed that the firms in an oligopolistic industry produce imperfect substitutes and that the whole demand function can be determined econometrically. In practice, however, such estimation is surrounded by considerable uncertainty. In particular, though time series may give a reasonable estimate of the slope of the pari passu demand curve—because the prices of the industry will often move together, due to common influences on cost—the cross elasticity of demand among individual products, and thus the slopes of the demand curves facing individual firms, will often be difficult to disentangle. The alternative approach that has recently gained favor in this field is to treat the slope of individual firm demand curves as an unknown, to be derived from the industry's observed behavior together with an assumption about market conduct.

Suppose, for instance, that we assume that an industry behaves in Bertrand fashion. We may have an econometric estimate for the slope of the pari passu demand curve,

$$\frac{p_x^B(x, p)}{1 - p_P^B(x, p)},$$

but we do not have reliable estimates for the slope of the firm-specific demand curve $p_x^B(x, P)$. What we do is use the first-order condition

$$\widetilde{MR}^B(x, p) = p + xp_x^B(x, p) = c$$

to infer a value for p_x^B. Then we calculate a value of p_P^B that makes this value consistent with the slope of the pari passu demand curve.

Similarly, if conduct is assumed to be Cournot, the slope of the pari passu demand curve may be written as

$$p_x^C(x, X) + p_X^C(x, X).$$

The slope of the ceteris paribus demand curve is inferred from the condition

$$\widetilde{MR}(x, x) = p + xp_x^C(x, x) = c,$$

and the value of p_X^C is then chosen to give the pari passu demand curve the right slope.

This procedure clearly avoids the conceptual problems associated with the conjectural variations approach. Competition is assumed to be either strict Cournot or strict Bertrand, with no awkward confusions between statics and dynamics, or between competition and collusion. The disadvantage is that the data is given no chance to tell us anything about market conduct. Whatever conduct is assumed is rationalized by the assumption that the cross elasticity is whatever would make the observed price optimal, so there is no opportunity to learn if the data is suggesting something other than the assumed conduct. In particular, there is no way to choose between Bertrand and Cournot. In practice, in the literature so far, this lack is dealt with either by a choice on a priori grounds or by calculating all analyses under both assumptions and comparing.

An important point to notice when the product differentiation approach is used is that because the demand function is left partially to be determined during the calibration procedure, the parameters of that function used when Bertrand behavior is assumed will be different from those when Cournot is assumed.

The Number of Firms

In our discussion up to this point we have assumed that the industry can actually be described as a collection of n symmetric firms. Real industries, however, do not look like that—think of the U.S. automobile or computer industry. The problem is therefore how to handle the fact of a size distribution of firms.

The right approach clearly would be to have a model that endogenously generates a size distribution, so that the data on actual size distribution would constitute useful information. In this ideal world one would also analyze alternative policies using a model that explicitly allows for a variety of firm sizes. The current state of theory, however, is one in which there is insufficient knowledge about the reasons for the existence of a size range of firms and in which tractable models depend on symmetry among firms.

The current employed alternative, then, is to use a hypothetical symmetric-firm industry as a kind of metaphor for the actual asymmetric industry under study. In defining this metaphor, it is clear that one should not simply use the actual number of firms in the industry—if these firms are greatly unequal in size, a simple count of firms will understate the effective degree of concentration. Thus the usual procedure is to model an industry with N actual nonsymmetric firms, as if it contained some smaller number n of symmetric firms. The number n is often set equal to the Herfindahl index

$$H = \left\{ \sum_{i=1}^{N} s_i^2 \right\}^{-1} = \left\{ \sum_{i=1}^{n} \left(\frac{1}{n} \right)^2 \right\}^{-1},$$

where s_i is firm i's actual share of sales. This index does not have a theoretical rationale but at least has the desirable properties of being increasing in the actual number of firms but decreasing in the size inequality among those firms.

Entry

As we emphasized in several of our chapters, assumptions about entry and exit of firms play a crucial role in many policy evaluations. Thus in empirical modeling something must be done about the modeling of entry and exit.

At this point there are two procedures available for handling this problem. The first is simply to treat the number of firms as invariant under alternative policies, in effect, to treat market structure as exogenously given. The alternative is to assume that there is free entry and exit that drives profits to zero.

Of course in real industries profits may not equal zero at any given point in time. With some costs of moving resources quickly, capital in an industry may at any given time be experiencing either abnormally high or abnormally low returns because of surprisingly favorable or unfavorable conditions. In calibrating free-entry models, however, the base period is assumed to be one in which profits are zero and therefore in which price equals average cost.

This may of course conflict directly with available data on cost. More usually, however, data on cost—like estimates of the demand function—will be less than precise, and the parameters of the cost function can be partially determined in the calibration procedure.

The usual case is the following: What the researcher starts with is an estimate from econometrics or industry sources of the degree of economies of scale in an industry. Let $C(x)$ be a total cost function, with $C'(x)$ a firm's marginal cost, and $C(x)/x$ its average cost. Then a useful inverse index of economies of scale is the elasticity of costs with respect to output:

$$v = \frac{C'(x)x}{C(x)} = \frac{C'(x)}{C(x)/x} = \frac{MC}{AC} \; .$$

That is, v is equal to the ratio of marginal to average costs. Suppose that we have an estimate of v, and we directly observe an industry's price p. Then, if we assume free entry that drives profits to zero, average cost must also equal p. This implies that marginal cost is equal to vp.

When comparative statics are then performed on a free-entry model, the number of firms is allowed to adjust until price again equals average cost.[2]

We have now reviewed the basic principles underlying the process of quantification of models of trade under imperfect competition. Our next step is to survey some of the main results from the quantification literature to date.

---

2. If profits are literally to be driven to zero, it is necessary to treat the number of firms as a continuous variable, ignoring the integer constraint. If the Herfindahl index is used for an initial n, this will already have been done in any case. However, it is also possible to respect the integer constraint. In this case entry proceeds until one more entrant will make profits negative. See the discussion of Baldwin and Krugman (1988) in section 8.3.

8.2 Models with Fixed Numbers of Firms

To illustrate the principles and problems of quantification in models where the number of firms is taken to be fixed, we consider an influential recent modeling effort. This is the pioneering work of Dixit (1988) who adopts the conjectural variations approach in his effort to model the effects of trade policy on the U.S. automobile industry.

Dixit's Model

Dixit's model of the U.S. auto industry has essentially the structure of the models we considered in chapter 6. There are assumed to be a number of U.S. firms producing a homogeneous product and a number of foreign firms producing a different homogeneous good that is an imperfect substitute for the U.S. good. The foreign firms are assumed both to have constant marginal cost and to be able to price discriminate between their home markets and the U.S. market; U.S. firms do not export. This means that the model can focus on the U.S. market alone and ignore what happens outside it. The setup allows for the possibility of gains from activist trade policy both from terms of trade improvements and from rent shifting. To separate these motives, Dixit considers the possibility of using two instruments, a specific tariff and a specific production subsidy.

The interdependent demand curves for U.S. and imported automobiles are assumed to arise from the quadratic utility function of a representative individual. This implies linear demand curves of the form

$$p_1 = a_1 - b_1 Q_1 - k Q_2,$$

$$p_2 = a_2 - b_2 Q_2 - k Q_1,$$

where 1 indicates the domestic good and 2 the imported good. Consumer surplus can be easily calculated from these demand functions.

The key assumption is about behavior. Suppose that there are n_1 domestic and n_2 foreign firms, and that within each group there is a fixed marginal cost. Thus the first-order condition for a domestic firm is

$$p_1 + \left(\frac{Q_1}{n_1}\right)\left(\frac{dp_1}{dq_1}\right) = c_1 - s,$$

where q_1 is the output of each firm, c_1 its marginal cost, s the subsidy, and (dp_1/dq_1) the *perceived* effect of a marginal output increase on the price. If all firms played Cournot, we would have $(dp_1/dq_1) = -b_1$. What Dixit does, instead, is to assume that

$$\left(\frac{dp_1}{dq_1}\right) = -V_1 b_1,$$

where V_1 is a conjectural variation parameter that can be different from one. Similarly, the foreign first-order condition is

$$p_2 + \left(\frac{Q_2}{n_2}\right)\left(\frac{dp_2}{dq_2}\right) = c_2 + t$$

and

$$\left(\frac{dp_2}{dq_2}\right) = -V_2 b_2,$$

with V_2 another conjectural variation parameter free to differ from one.

It is important to notice that this is not a fully general conjectural variations setup. In principle, there could be *four* CV (conjectural variations) parameters, since U.S. firms might have conjectures about how foreign firms respond, and vice versa. In calibrating to a static equilibrium, of course, this makes no difference: two CV parameters are sufficient to match the data. In comparative statics exercises, however, the implicit assumption that the cross conjectures are zero may make some difference.

In doing policy exercises, Dixit assumes that the conjectures remain constant. The lack of a good rationale for this, as well as the reasons for assuming it anyway, were discussed in the previous section.

Calibration
In Dixit's approach to calibration everything except the conjectural variations parameters are taken from outside estimates. Econometric estimates of the elasticity of demand for automobiles and the cross elasticity of demand for domestic and foreign autos are used to calibrate the demand system (with constant terms chosen to reproduce actual sales in a base period). The marginal cost of firms is estimated from data on firms by assuming that it is equal to the average variable production cost. The number of firms is estimated

from market share data using the Herfindahl index discussed earlier. This leaves only two parameters, V_1 and V_2. However, given the first-order conditions, once actual prices and quantities are given, and the slope of the demand curve and the number of firms-equivalent are assumed, it is possible to solve directly for the conjectures as

$$V_1 = \frac{p_1 - c_1 + s}{(Q_1/n_1)b_1},$$

$$V_2 = \frac{p_2 - c_2 - t}{(Q_2/n_2)b_2}.$$

Results

The calibration exercise produces conjectural variations that jump around depending on which year is used as a base—another reason for caution in making too much of the results. However, in general, Japanese firms end up with a V_2 that is approximately equal to 1 so that Cournot behavior is apparently a reasonable approximation. However, U.S. firms end up with a V_1 that is considerably less than one.[3] That is, they are more competitive than Cournot. (But since price lies above marginal cost and the U.S. good is assumed to be homogeneous, they are less competitive than Bertrand.)

Given these results, it is next possible to solve for optimal policies. Quantitatively, these results depend on the base year used for calibration, but qualitatively they are fairly robust. In essence, three results emerge:

1. When a tariff is the only instrument available, the optimal tariff rate is positive, ranging from about 8 to 17 percent.

2. When a subsidy is available as well, a small positive subsidy turns out to be optimal, and the optimal tariff is reduced somewhat.

3. In any case the gains from either a tariff or a subsidy alone seem small, and the gains from a combined optimal policy, though larger, are still quite small.

---

3. Actually, Dixit states his results in terms of "firms equivalent" instead of V_i—that is, he normalizes V_i to 1 and finds the n_i that would lead to the observed price. This makes no difference, except that it facilitates statement of one issue that arises: that of how to treat the multidivisional structure of U.S. firms. If the separate divisions of U.S. firms are assumed to make independent output and/or pricing decisions, n_1 becomes much larger and correspondingly the estimate V_1 becomes larger.

Table 8.1 gives representative results from Dixit's calibration for 1980. The column labeled "MFN tariff" represents the actual tariff that the United States was applying; this, rather than free trade, was used as a base. The successive columns show the results of an optimal tariff when the tariff is used alone, an optimal subsidy when this is used alone, and the optimal combined tax and subsidy policy. Two further points may be noted from the table. First, a subsidy is much more beneficial than a tariff when each is used alone, and the marginal gain from adding a tariff to a subsidy is even smaller than the gain from a tariff alone. Thus the potential gains from policy have much more to do with the gap between price and marginal cost than with trade issues per se.

Second, the redistribution of income is large compared with the net gains. For example, in the tariff-alone case consumers experience losses that are more than seven times as large as the overall gain. Although this is offset by gains in government revenue and profits, obvious questions are raised about the political economy of such a policy. Will the government really be indifferent to such changes in income distribution? Won't there be a danger that government analysis will be biased by the desire to convey benefits or avoid losses to particular groups?

Table 8.1
Policy calculations for the U.S. auto industry, 1979

	MFN tariff	Optimum tariff	Optimum subsidy	Optimum tariff and subsidy
Tariff	100	570	0	408
Subsidy	0	0	673	611
Profit	4.751	4.663	5.645	5.627
Consumer surplus	27.918	27.310	33.463	32.421
Tariff revenue	0.162	0.758	0	0.539
Subsidy cost	0	0	6.206	5.627
U.S. welfare	32.651	32.731	32.902	32.960
Gain over MFN	0	0.080	0.251	0.309

Source: Dixit (1988), p. 158.
Note: Tariff and subsidy rates are measured in $/auto. All other variables are measured in $billion.

8.3 Models with Free Entry

Ideally, quantitative models of imperfect competition would estimate the conditions of entry in the same way that other elements of the model are estimated, as part of the calibration. In practice, this is not yet something that has been done. Instead, entry is either assumed to be blockaded or free, and this is simply imposed. The choice may be made on the basis of intuition about the industry—Dixit clearly felt that a fixed-entry description of the U.S. auto industry was more realistic than a model in which changes in trade policy might lead to changes in the number of firms, even though his model tells us nothing about why the dominance of the Big Three has been so stable for decades. Conversely, for the case of semiconductors, studied by Baldwin and Krugman (1988), a fixed-number-of-firms assumption clearly seems absurd: the industry is too dynamic and changeable to be dominated by a stable group of oligopolists, and indeed each successive round of competition has narrowed the field of competitors so that there always appear to be more potential producers than can in fact enter profitably.

An alternative, less respectable justification for the choice of entry assumption is that such an assumption can substitute for data. Suppose that the investigator has a reasonable estimate of marginal cost but no good estimate of economies of scale. Then a no-entry model can be calibrated, but a free-entry model cannot. If the converse is true—the investigator has an estimate of scale economies but no estimate of marginal cost—then a free entry model can be calibrated but a fixed-numbers model cannot. This is not the way one would like to do quantitative economics, but the effort to get at least suggestive quantitative results has forced even the most careful researchers into awkward compromises.

In this section we describe two examples of free-entry quantitative models: the Baldwin and Krugman (1988) semiconductor study and the recent work by Venables and Smith (1987, 1988) on European integration.

The Baldwin-Krugman Model

The semiconductor industry is one in which competition takes a clear product cycle form; every four or five years a product is superseded by a superior substitute so that firms are in effect required to reenter their own market. When new products are introduced, they are reputedly subject to a steep learning curve.

The basis of the Baldwin-Krugman study is the recognition that learning economies at the level of the firm represents a kind of increasing returns. Indeed under some circumstances, a learning curve model is essentially isomorphic to a static model with down-ward-sloping average and marginal cost. Baldwin and Krugman es-sentially follow the formulation of Spence (1981), in which this equivalence is shown, and collapse the product cycle into a one-shot static competitive game.

The equivalence may be seen as follows: Consider a firm that plans to produce a good over a period of length T, where T is sufficiently short that the firm can ignore discounting. The firm's rate of pro-duction at any point in time t is $x(t)$; its instantaneous production costs are assumed to be

$$C(t) = x(t)c[K(t)], \qquad c' < 0,$$

where $K(t)$ is cumulative production to date:

$$K(t) = \int_0^t x(\tau)d\tau. \tag{8.8}$$

Thus the more a firm has produced, the lower its cost of further production.

What Spence pointed out is that the true marginal cost facing a firm at any point in time combines two components: the direct mar-ginal production cost and the effect of higher production now in reducing future costs of production.[4] This true marginal cost may be written as

$$\mu(t) = c[K(t)] + \int_t^T x(\tau)c'[K(\tau)]d\tau,$$

where the second term represents the effects on future costs. In this calculation the interest rate is taken to equal zero.

---

4. The formulation described here is valid only if firms either must precommit them-selves to a production path or ignore the effect of their actions on the subsequent production paths of other firms. If this is not the case, the decision by a firm on how much to produce currently becomes a strategic move that affects the subsequent game among firms, greatly complicating the calculation of behavior (see Fudenberg and Tirole 1983). In Baldwin and Krugman (1988) the assumption is made that the tech-nology of production imposes a precommitment.

Now we ask how true marginal cost μ changes over time. This change contains two elements. Direct marginal cost falls over time as the efficiency of production rises, but the indirect benefit of adding experience falls as the end of the product cycle comes closer. Differentiating with respect to time, and making use of (8.8), we find $\dot{\mu} = 0$. Thus it turns out that these two effects precisely offset one another: true marginal costs are flat through the product cycle.

Now notice that for output at time T, at the end of the product cycle, $\mu = c$: direct and economic marginal costs coincide. What we have therefore learned is that over the whole of the cycle true marginal cost is the same as the direct marginal cost of the last unit produced. In other words, firms should make decisions as if they simply had a downward-sloping marginal cost curve in terms of the aggregate production over the product cycle.

In the semiconductor industry there is widespread acceptance of the view that costs follow fairly closely a learning curve of the form $c = AK^{-\lambda}$, with λ in the range 0.2 to 0.4; Baldwin and Krugman use an estimate of $\lambda = 0.28$. This instantaneous cost may be thought of as arising from a total cost function of the form

$$C = (1 - \lambda)^{-1}AK^{1-\lambda}.$$

The average cost of production over the product cycle is

$$\frac{C}{K(T)} = (1 - \lambda)^{-1}AK(T)^{-\lambda},$$

whereas the marginal cost of production at the end of the product cycle is

$$c[K(T)] = AK(T)^{-\lambda}.$$

Hence the ratio of marginal cost to average, which as we have seen is also the elasticity of cost with respect to output, is $\nu = 1 - \lambda = 0.72$. This implies that the strong learning effects in semiconductors are de factor a source of very strong economies of scale.

The Baldwin-Krugman study examines the competition in one particular kind of semiconductor product, dynamic random access memories, for one generation, the 16K RAM (whose product cycle ran roughly from 1978 to 1983). Industry sources describe 16K RAMs as a "commodity" chip, one that is essentially a standardized product; thus chips manufactured in Japan and the United States are assumed to be perfect substitutes.

The structure of the model is that of segmented market competition, as described in chapter 8. The United States and Japan are treated as separable markets, with firms separately commiting deliveries to each market; as a result there is a possibility of intraindustry trade in RAMs (there actually was some two-way trade).

The model is calibrated using the assumption of free entry and the conjectural variations approach. First, average revenue net of transport cost was assumed equal to average cost for firms in each country—the zero-profits assumption. This, together with the assumed learning curve elasticity, gave an estimate of marginal cost for firms.

The study then needed to estimate four conjectural variations: that of U.S. firms in their home market, of Japanese firms in the U.S. market, of Japanese firms in the Japanese market, and of U.S. firms in the Japanese market. The first three of these were estimated using price-cost margins. For example, the conjectural variation of U.S. firms in their own market, V_{UU}, may be determined by noting that

$$P_U = \left(\frac{\epsilon}{\epsilon - \sigma_{UU}V_{UU}/n}\right) MC_U,$$

where P_U is the price of chips in the U.S. market, ϵ the elasticity of market demand, σ_{UU} the share of U.S. firms in their home market, n the number of U.S. firms-equivalent, and MC_U the marginal cost of U.S. firms.

The fourth conjectural variation, that of U.S. firms in the Japanese market, could not be similarly estimated. The reason is the anecdotal evidence that the Japanese market was tacitly closed to U.S. chips. This was represented in the model by an implicit tariff on U.S. sales in Japan; this implied an equation of the form

$$P_J = \left(\frac{\epsilon}{\epsilon - \sigma_{UJ}V_{UJ}/n}\right) (1 + \tau)(1 + \phi)MC_U,$$

where ϕ was the transportation cost and τ the implicit tariff. This implies that the conjectural variation cannot be identified without some other way of tying down the implicit tariff, or conversely. The somewhat unsatisfactory answer offered was to assume that $V_{UJ} = V_{UU}$, that is, that U.S. firms behave the same in the Japanese market as they do at home.

The calibration exercise produced the result that conjectural variations were all substantially larger than one—that is, the market was definitely less competitive than Cournot (and a fortiori less competitive than Bertrand). This result is somewhat disturbing and puts the validity of the model in considerable question—a question further reinforced by doubts about whether the dynamics of such a complex industry can be adequately modeled so crudely. Nevertheless, the model produced highly suggestive results.

Results

The key question asked of the model was, How much difference did the apparent Japanese market closure make? This question actually has two components. First is the positive question of effects on market shares and trade patterns. Evidently, this model of semiconductors is in the class of "import protection as export promotion" models (see Krugman 1984) in which it is possible that Japanese exports are the result of a protected domestic market. The other question is whether the closed market actually benefited Japan.

Table 8.2 shows the results of three calculations. The first column shows a base case that is meant to represent the actual competition in RAMs; in this base case the implicit closure of Japan's market is represented by a tariff rate of 0.2637. The second column shows what happens when this tariff is removed. The third shows a "trade war," in which both countries impose 100 percent tariffs that completely choke off trade.

The results suggest a crucial nontraditional effect of protection on the pattern of specialization but a more conventional result with regard to welfare. When the equilibrium is calculated without the implicit Japanese tariff, the Japanese industry—which was a net exporter in actuality—simply disappears. That is, no firms can profitably enter. Meanwhile an extra U.S. firm enters. Thus the model suggests a strong export-promoting effect of protection.

The reason for this result is the following: According to the calibration, Japanese firms were found to have a somewhat higher inherent cost than U.S. firms—that is, in the cost function $c = AK^{-\lambda}$ Japanese firms had a somewhat higher A than U.S. firms. As a result of protection, however, Japanese firms were able to survive and indeed to have sufficiently long production runs to end up with slightly lower average and marginal costs than their U.S. rivals. When the model is run with an open Japanese market, the higher-cost Japanese firms cannot enter profitably, and so the industry remains entirely U.S. based, with Japan importing all of its demand.

Table 8.2
Simulation results for semiconductor competition

	Base case	Free trade	Trade war
Welfare[a]			
United States	1,651.8	1,828.5	1,636.7
Japan	698.4	738.9	225.6
Consumer surplus[a]			
United States	1,651.8	1,822.5	1,636.7
Japan	698.6	738.9	225.6
Price[b]			
United States	1.47	1.30	1.49
Japan	1.47	1.37	2.19
Profit[a]			
United States	0	6	0
Japan	0	0	0
Import shares			
United States in Japan	0.14	1.0	0
Japan in United States	0.19	0	0
Number of firms			
United States	6	7	7
Japan	3	0	5

Source: Baldwin and Krugman (1988), table 5, corrected by authors.
a. In millions of dollars.
b. In dollars per unit.

We know from the theoretical models in chapter 7 that protection in this kind of market could be a successful beggar-thy-neighbor policy. In this exercise, however, it does not turn out to be one. The counterfactual simulation in which Japan does not protect its domestic market yields higher welfare in both the United States and Japan. Thus, although the model indicates the possibility of radically different effects of trade policy from conventional ones, it does not provide any support for protection as being in the protecting country's interest.

Also the model indicates that a trade war is mutually immiserizing. Since even unilateral Japanese protection is not welfare improving for Japan, however, the model does not yield a Prisoner's Dilemma situation.

The Smith-Venables Model

Venables and Smith (1986, 1987, 1988) have developed a framework for quantifying the effects of trade policy in Europe that combines Dixit-style quantification with a differentiated-product approach. The model is quite complex and not easily summarized; all that we do here is to describe briefly its character and overall results.

The basic idea of the model is that each firm produces a number of "models" (differentiated products). There are both economies of scale—the larger the production of a given model, the lower is its average cost—and economies of scope—the more models a firm produces, the lower is its average cost. Thus competition among firms takes place at two levels. At the lower level firms choose either the prices or outputs of models; at the upper level the firms choose the number of models to produce. The model also includes a degree of market segmentation, with firms free to choose prices that differ across markets.

The calibration of the model to this two-level competition represents a mixture of the two methods described in the simplified example in section 8.1 Venables and Smith have direct evidence on prices and marginal costs so that they must reproduce actual pricing behavior; they also assume that the observed data represents a zero-profit situation. To reproduce the observed price-marginal cost margin, they impose the assumption of either Cournot or Bertrand behavior at the lower level; then they calculate the implied elasticity of substitution among goods. To reconcile the model with zero profitability, they follow a conjectural variations approach at the upper level of competition.

Venables and Smith (1986) uses their modeling approach for an exercise similar to Dixit's: to look for optimal trade policies for several U.K. industries. Broadly speaking, their results are similar in character to Dixit's: some protection is found to be superior to free trade, but the optimal tariffs are small and the potential benefits very small. The difference is that tariffs are in their approach found to be beneficial, even with free entry that eliminates profits, because they can improve the tariff-imposing country's terms of trade (see chapter 7). An interesting and reassuring feature of the Venables-Smith results is that neither the choice between Bertrand and Cournot competition nor the assumption made about entry seems to be critical for their conclusions.

Table 8.3
Effects of a 5 percent tariff on appliances under alternative assumptions
(changes from base case, million 1982 ECU)

	No entry	Free entry
Cournot		
Consumer surplus	−47.6	2.8
Profits	47.9	0
Government revenue	28.9	22.7
Welfare[a]	1.3	1.1
Bertrand		
Consumer surplus	−33.3	2.2
Profits	21.6	0
Government revenue	31.8	28.4
Welfare[a]	0.9	1.3

Source: Venables and Smith (1987), table 3.
a. As percentage of base consumption.

Table 8.3 shows a sample table for the electrical appliances industry. Four cases are distinguished: behavior is assumed to be either
Cournot or Bertrand, and the number of firms and products is assumed to be either completely fixed or completely flexible.[5] We see
that the result of a small welfare gain for the UK obtains under all
four, and that the size of the gain is almost the same in each case.
The main difference is in distributional impacts. With restricted entry
there are large redistributional effects, as firms and government gain
while consumers lose. In the free-entry case consumers actually gain
slightly (because of the home market effect, as analyzed in chapter
7), firms earn zero profits throughout, and the government gains
revenue. In this case the nature of competition seems to make little
difference.

Venables and Smith (1988) have also considered the effects of
removal of remaining obstacles to trade within Europe, modeled as
a reduction in transportation costs. For the most part the industrial
organization effects of this opening reinforce the more conventional
gains. However, in the cement industry case, where transport costs
are very high in any case, a small reduction in transport costs actually

5. Venables and Smith also consider an intermediate case in which firms can change
the number of products they offer but cannot enter or exit. We omit the results here
to avoid clutter, but they are generally intermediate between the free-entry and no-
entry cases.

reduced welfare. This result corresponds to the possibility of welfare-reducing trade in the presence of segmented markets described in Helpman and Krugman (1985, ch. 5).

8.4 General Equilibrium Modeling

The major effort at the general equilibrium application of industrial organization concepts to international trade is the work of Harris and Cox (1984) on U.S.-Canadian trade.

At the industry level the Harris-Cox model is in the same general class as the models already discussed. The main distinctive (and controversial) feature is the attempt to make a compromise between noncooperative pricing behavior and collusion. They offer two pricing schemes: one based on perceived elasticity of demand, and one in which a collusive domestic industry is limited in its price by the threat of foreign competition. Actual price is then assumed to be determined by an average of these two schemes—something that lacks a fully described rationale. The idea of prices limited by foreign prices is important because it gives protection a strong, direct role in determining the effective competitiveness of the domestic market.

The main distinctive feature of the Harris-Cox approach, however, is that industrial organization is overlaid on a general equilibrium model of trade in which conventional comparative advantage also plays a role. Thus the model imposes overall resource constraints and can be compared with constant returns, perfect competition computable general equilibrium models.

The main result of the Harris-Cox model is its implication that trade liberalization will lead to rationalization through exit, significantly longer production runs, lower fixed costs, and hence greater efficiency in the manufacturing sector. The model finds that a unilateral Canadian move to free trade, which previous studies had found created only minor gains, would, instead, produce fairly substantial benefits for Canada. A free trade pact with the United States would produce welfare gains of almost 9 percent of GNP, more than twice as large as anything estimated using conventional models.

There is also an interesting positive prediction: the model shows Canada shifting from an importer to an exporter of manufactured goods on net as a result of trade liberalization, rather than intensifying its original pattern of specialization. The reason presumably is the home market effect on the location of production of goods pro-duced subject to economies of scale. As long as there are barriers to trade between the United States and Canada, the United States, being the larger market, is the preferred location for the production of any goods subject to economies of scale, chiefly manufactures. With the barriers gone, the market size matters less (see Helpman and Krug-man 1985, ch. 10), and in the Harris-Cox model the effect is actually to reverse the pattern of interindustry trade.

8.5 Conclusions

The efforts to produce quantitative models of trade policy under imperfect competition are still few in number and tentative in char-acter. The main message of the work so far may be just how difficult it is to apply the kind of theoretical analysis that has proliferated in recent years; all of the work so far has depended on chains of as-sumptions that represent reasonable research strategy but that one would hesitate to rely on for actual policymaking. However, several suggestive results do seem to emerge.

First is the result that mild protection can—if it is not retaliated against—raise national welfare, and it seems to be fairly robust. We have seen in various chapters that arguments in favor of aggressive trade policies are contingent on assumptions about behavior and entry. In the empirical work to date that problem seems less severe than one might have expected, at least for tariffs. Small tariffs seem to yield gains in a variety of models.

Second, the gains from such policy are small. Nothing in the quantitative analysis to date provides a justification for sweeping claims that imperfect markets offer large gains to sophisticated inter-vention, still less that neo-mercantilist policies can be the key to rapid economic growth. If there are really large benefits from trade inter-vention, they must lie in sources other than imperfect competition alone.

Third, although the quantification exercises offer some support for unilateral protectionism, they also suggest that the gains from trade are larger than one would have previously supposed and that the costs of mutual protection are magnified by industrial organization effects. In fact, the principal effect of the new models on practical policy discussion has been to reinforce arguments in favor of trade liberalization: the work of Harris and Cox has been used to argue for a Canadian-U.S. trade pact, and more recently the work of Venables and Smith has been used in support of the variety of European liberalization measures summarized under the heading of "1992."

Clearly, there is a great deal of work to be done in this area. A gradual accumulation of industry case studies will certainly help give the theoretical analysis less of an abstract feel. We may also hope that eventually improved methodologies of work in this area will be developed and also that theoretical models will improve to the point that they can be fitted to the data with less strain.

References

Baldwin, Richard, and Krugman, Paul R. (1988). "Market access and international competition: A simulation study of 16K Random Access Memories." In Robert Feenstra (ed.), *Empirical Methods for International Trade*. Cambridge, MA: MIT Press.

Cox, David, and Harris, Richard (1985). "Trade liberalization and industrial organisation: Some estimates for Canada." *Journal of Political Economy* 93: 115–145.

Dixit, Avinash (1988). "Optimal trade and industrial policies for the US automobile industry." In Robert Feenstra (ed.), *Empirical Methods for International Trade*. Cambridge, MA: MIT Press.

Eaton, Jonathan, and Grossman, Gene M. (1986). "Optimal trade and industrial policy under oligopoly." *Quarterly Journal of Economics* 101: 383–406.

Fudenberg, Drew, and Tirole, Jean, (1983), "Learning-by-doing and market performance." *Bell Journal of Economics* 14: 522–530.

Harris, Richard, with Cox, David (1984). *Trade, Industrial Policy, and Canadian Manufacturing*. Toronto: Ontario Economic Council.

Helpman, Elhanan, and Krugman, Paul R. (1985). *Market Structure and Foreign Trade*. Cambridge, MA: MIT Press.

Krugman, Paul R. (1984). "Import protection as export promotion." In Henryk Kierzkowski (ed.), *Monopolistic Competition and International Trade*. Oxford: Blackwell.

Spence, Michael E. (1981). "The learning curve and competition." *Bell Journal of Economics* 12: 49–70.

Tirole, Jean (1988). *The Theory of Industrial Organization*. Cambridge, MA: MIT Press.

Venables, Anthony, and Smith, Alasdair M. (1986). "Trade and industrial policy under imperfect competition." *Economic Policy* 1: 622–672.

Venables, Anthony, and Smith, Alasdair M. (1987). "Trade and industrial policy: Some simulations for EEC manufacturing." Presented at Conference on Empirical Studies of Strategic Trade Policy. Cambridge, MA, September 17–18.

Venables, Anthony, and Smith, Alasdair M. (1988). "Completing the internal market in the European Community: Some industry simulations." *European Economic Review*, forthcoming.

9 Conclusions

By its nature the material presented in this book does not lend itself to any easy summary. Oligopolies are inherently capable of a greater range of behavior than atomistically competitive industries—there is only one way to be perfect, but many ways to be imperfect. Even though we have made extreme simplifying assumptions throughout, a main message of this book is how many things can happen once the assumption of perfect competition is lifted.

Nevertheless, some basic themes do emerge from the contrast between the analysis presented here and conventional analysis of trade policy. Three themes in particular strike us as worth reemphasizing.

First, we have found that a number of seemingly disparate issues in this area can be addressed using two basic tools. One of these is the concept of perceived marginal revenue. In many of our models the whole issue of market structure reduces to the construction of the perceived marginal revenue curve. The other is the assessment of welfare consequences of a small change in policy using "wedges"—divergences from conditions that would hold in a perfectly efficient economy (such as the difference between the domestic producer price and marginal cost of production, or the difference between true marginal revenue and marginal cost for exports). The repeated usefulness of these two concepts gives the book a certain degree of methodological unity.

Second, a recurrent theme in the market structures treated here is that the effects of trade policy on output, prices, and trade may be quite different from what an intuition schooled in perfect competition leads one to expect. Our findings contain many perverse results: protection that reduces domestic output, subsidies to imports that improve the terms of trade, and tariffs that lower domestic prices.

Thus the theory of trade policy under imperfect competition suggests that market structure will be crucial in making predictions about policy effects.

Third, although the predicted impacts of trade policies are non-conventional, the welfare economics of these policies are less so. Free trade is rarely the optimal policy under oligopoly, but no clear alternative emerges. The case for any particular deviation from free trade is highly sensitive to assumptions about market structure and behavior, and the quantitative importance of potential gains from intervention is also doubtful.

We now address each of these themes in somewhat more detail.

9.1 Methodology

At first glance the burgeoning literature on trade policy under imperfect competition seems to offer a limitless profusion of models and approaches. One of the aims of this book was to cut down on this variety by offering some common explanations and tools of analysis. In most of the models studied here, we found it possible to use the same basic approach to determination of equilibrium and the assessment of welfare.

Our analysis led us into repeated use of the concept of perceived marginal revenue. In noncooperative models the effects of differences in market structure, and to an important extent of differences in behavior, can be captured by differences in perceived marginal revenue. In a price-taking industry perceived marginal revenue is simply the price—and thus the perceived marginal revenue curve for the industry is simply the demand curve. In a monopoly marginal revenue is less than the price because the firm knows that an effort to increase sales will depress revenue on inframarginal units. In an oligopoly each firm typically perceives itself as facing a marginal revenue that lies between the price and the marginal revenue that a monopolist would face. The reasons are apparent. Perceived marginal revenue lies below the demand curve because firms, not being price-takers, are concerned about the effects of an increase in deliveries on their inframarginal sales, but it lies above the industry marginal revenue because each individual firm is unconcerned about the impact it has on the revenue of other firms.

We were able to make extensive use of the perceived marginal revenue curve technique in chapters 3 and 4 where it helped us see when insights based on monopoly behavior carried over to oligopoly and when they did not. For example, the proposition that a quota reduces domestic output as compared with a tariff, because it leads to a steeper demand curve and hence lower marginal revenue, remains true for an oligopoly, whose perceived marginal revenue is a weighted average of the demand and true marginal revenue curves. On the other hand, the proposition that foreigners will raise their prices to appropriate all rents from an import quota applies to a foreign monopoly but needs to be qualified for an oligopoly because for an oligopoly marginal revenue no longer drops to zero when a quota is binding; firms can still poach customers from each other.

Perhaps more surprisingly, we found the perceived marginal revenue technique useful even in the strategic analysis of chapter 5. Here the important distinction is between an ex ante or true marginal revenue curve—what the domestic industry would face if it could precommit to any given level of output—and the perceived marginal revenue of firms that take foreign output or price as given. The popular argument that strategic considerations favor an aggressive export policy rests on the proposition that ex ante marginal revenue exceeds perceived due to deterrence effects: if foreigners know that we are committed to produce more, they will produce less. What the analysis in these terms lets us immediately see is that other factors pull in the opposite direction. Competition among domestic firms raises perceived marginal revenue relative to true marginal revenue; Bertrand behavior reverses the deterrent effect; even if ex ante marginal revenue is higher than firms' perception, an industry must compete for resources with other industries for which the same may be true.

About our welfare analysis less, perhaps, needs to be said. We maintained the assumption that the economy outside the sector being studied can be viewed as undistorted so that prices and costs represent true social opportunities. Given this assumption, however, the welfare effects of any small policy change can arise only from reducing or aggravating the distortions already present in a market, on one side, or altering the terms of trade, on the other.

The important point about this approach is that it focuses attention on the nature of the distortions inherent in imperfect competition. The most basic, of course, is the difference between price and marginal cost; this always offers a potential wedge for government action because consumers tend to buy too few domestic products. The first-best policy to correct this distortion, however, is to eliminate it, whether by somehow forcing marginal cost pricing on the part of firms or by subsidizing domestic consumption of domestic goods. The important point about such a first-best solution is that it is not, in essence, a trade policy per se. Thus by focusing on the distortions, we get a useful caution against putting too much weight on the case for trade policies, which can only be second-best answers, as opposed to more general industrial policy. For this reason the usefulness of trade policy is limited, and the design of a welfare-improving policy requires detailed information about the economy.

The other possible source of gains from trade policy is via the terms of trade. The possibility of terms of trade gains from protection is, of course, a part of the standard analysis described in chapter 2. What is different here is the increased range of possibilities. In competitive markets taxes on trade (tariffs or export taxes) can improve the terms of trade, but only if a country is large in world markets. In imperfectly competitive markets a small country may still be able to improve its terms of trade and an improvement in the terms of trade may require such seemingly perverse policies as an import subsidy.

These extra possibilities arise because the effects of trade policy in imperfectly competitive markets are more complex than in competitive markets and sometimes seemingly perverse. This, then, brings us to our next general theme: the often surprising impacts of trade policy under imperfect competition.

9.2 Surprising Effects of Policy

In the days when the theory of trade policy under perfect competition was being developed, seemingly paradoxical results got wide attention. This was partly because they were interesting intellectual puzzles but also because the seeming paradoxes helped to highlight the deep structure of the models. Thus Metzler's (1949) demonstration that a tariff can actually lower the internal relative price of the protected good and Bhagwati's (1958) result that economic growth can actually reduce the growing country's welfare were useful in forcing an appreciation of the underlying structure of the standard trade model.

The theory of trade policy under imperfect competition is full of paradoxes. To name only a few of the ones demonstrated in this book, a tariff or import quota may reduce the output of the protected industry (chapter 3), an import subsidy may improve the terms of trade (chapter 4), an export subsidy may raise the subsidized firm's profits by more than the subsidy itself (chapter 5), protection can raise the profits of foreign as well as domestic firms (chapter 6), and a tariff can reduce internal prices (chapter 7).

The basic reason for this prevalence of unusual results is that under imperfect competition firms react to more aspects of their situation than they do under perfect competition. Instead of simply setting marginal cost equal to the price, firms set it equal to perceived marginal revenue. Perceived marginal revenue, however, is affected in complex ways by trade policy, since it depends not only on the slope of the demand curve but also on the nature of the other firms' reactions. Thus it should not be a surprise to find that imperfectly competitive markets behave quite differently from the ways that competitive analysis has led us to expect.

This looks like an important point. Many markets are in fact imperfectly competitive. The limited work on quantifying the effects of trade policy in such markets, as described in chapter 8, does confirm the theoretical presumption that nonstandard impacts of policy will be common. Thus economists need to be cautious in their predictions of policy effects. The standard practice has been to assume that competitive models give more or less correct predictions, needing only a little touching up to apply to the oligopolies that are the concern of most actual trade policies. The theory surveyed here suggests otherwise. The evaluation of trade policy should take imperfect competition into account from the start.

The immediate question that follows from this, however, is whether this means a complete rethinking of trade policy as well. Is the case for free trade, so long a central economic tenet, now invalidated? Despite what we have said about the effects of trade policy, we do not think so.

9.3 The Welfare Effects of Trade Policy

Free trade is not optimal in imperfectly competitive industries. At minimum, such industries must have prices not equal to marginal cost; this divergence creates a second-best justification for some kind of trade policy. However, free trade is often not optimal in competitive sectors either. External economies, factor market distortions, and for that matter the wedges associated with various taxes are pervasive in any real-world economy. A key question about the new trade theory is whether it gives rise to any systematic new reason to reject free trade.

The answer appears to be no. Although some models can be used to support neo-mercantilist policies—tariffs to improve the terms of trade or export subsidies to give firms a strategic advantage—slight variations on these models eliminate or even reverse their conclusions. No blanket vindication of aggressive trade policies emerges from the analysis, nor does it seem likely that a real-world government would be able to decide which model is most relevant. The design of an advantageous trade policy requires information of a kind that is simply not available.

Also the theoretical analysis pinpoints the source of potential gain in the distortions that are associated with imperfect competition. Although these distortions are inevitable, one needs to ask how large they are. Price exceeds marginal cost—but by how much? Ex ante or true marginal revenue may exceed perceived marginal revenue, but how large can this divergence be? It is possible to believe that imperfect competition is pervasive while at the same time believing that the imperfections associated with it are fairly modest and the gains from optimal deviations from free trade small. Again, the quantitative work reported in chapter 8 seems to confirm this. One can always do better than free trade, but the optimal tariffs or subsidies seem to be small, the potential gains tiny, and there is plenty of room for policy errors that may lead to eventual losses rather than gains.

The political economy of trade policy is therefore not changed as much by the new models as is the description of its effects. No sophisticated analyst ever thought that free trade was literally optimal for a single country. The case for free trade has always rested on an argument that it represents a good rule of thumb given uncertainty about the alternatives, realistic appreciation of the difficulties of managing political intervention, and the need to avoid trade wars.

9.4 Where Do We Go from Here?

Clearly the analysis of trade policy under imperfect competition is far from a finished product. No doubt the directions taken by the field may surprise us, just as the sudden emergence of the field ten years ago surprised many. However, we see four main areas in which there is obvious room for more productive work.

First, we need better models of market structure. The workhorse models of the theoretical analysis assume symmetric industries consisting of equal-size firms. Real industries have a size distribution, an awkward fact that receives an awkward treatment in quantitative work. It would add greatly to the persuasiveness of models if the size distribution of firms could be made endogenous and hence meaningful.

Second, we need to address the problem of cooperative behavior better. The idea that repeated games may support cooperative behavior has received wide attention but has led to few useful models. Our discussion in chapter 3 showed that such models could have very different results from noncooperative models, but our exercise there was provocative rather than convincing. Eventually, we want to have models in which the real-world activities of oligopolists, who accept price leaders, signal to each other, and sometimes meet clandestinely in motel rooms, have some counterpart.

Third, we also need to incorporate real dynamics. There are several trade models in which firms invest over time in capital and/or R&D, but basically the implications of dynamics for trade policy are still little understood. For example, recent work by Grossman and Helpman (1988) has shown that in the presence of dynamic economies of scale trade policy can change the long-run rate of growth. In this type of an environment the dynamic effects of trade policy can be much larger than the static effects considered in this book. We do not know, however, how large this difference can be.

Finally, the field needs more quantification. Since the possible range of behavior in the new models is so wide, above all we need to confront the models with data in order to narrow the possibilities. The work reported in chapter 8 is a good and exciting start, but much more needs to be done.

This is a large agenda. However, surely given the history of recent research in international trade one cannot be discouraged. Only a decade ago many if not most of the subjects treated in this book were widely regarded as intractable. Instead, it has turned out that they may be approached with models that are not only comprehensible but also simple and elegant—so much so that it is hard to believe that one was ever confused. It is the mark of really good theory that it offers insights that are startling at first yet seem obvious once fully absorbed.

References

Bhagwati, Jagdish N. (1958). "Immizerizing growth: A geometrical note." *Review of Economic Studies* 25: 201–205.

Grossman, Gene M., and Helpman, Elhanan (1988). "Comparative advantage and long run growth." Mimeo.

Metzler, Lloyd (1949). "Tariffs, the terms of trade, and the distribution of national income." *Journal of Political Economy* 57: 1–29.

Index